Sri Lanka
A Victor's Peace

2009 to 2019

Ana Pararajasingham

Monitor Publications

Published by Monitor Publications, Sydney, September 2019

Copyright@ Ana Pararajasingham

ISBN No: 978-0-6486722-0-3

Contents

Acknowledgements v

Foreword vii

Introduction xi

The International Dimensions of the Conflict in Sri Lanka 1

A Safer Place for Tamils 9

Sri Lanka: In the Eye of the Storm 13

Frances Harrisons' Still Counting the Dead 17

Required: A Sri Lanka Policy 20

Colombo's Military Build-Up: A Strategy of Deterrence 26

Sri Lanka's Re-embrace of China Leaves India
    out in the Cold 30

The Tamil Nadu Factor: Demanding Justice for
    Genocide in Sri Lanka 35

Extension Given to Probe Sri Lanka's War
    Crimes is No Surprise 40

The Politics of Persuasion-An Evaluation 44

Sri Lanka: Sovereignty Compromised 56

Trincomalee Beckons: Is New Delhi Becoming Assertive? 60

Realpolitik Not Humanitarian Concerns
    Will Decide Myanmar's Future 65

Sri Lankan Constitution: The Strategy of Doublespeak 70

Sri Lanka's Proposed Constitution Comes Under Attack....75

India's Regional Power Credentials under Threat by China....79

Sri Lankan Regime Backing Away from
    Conflict Resolution Vows... 84

Hindutva takes on Tamil Nationalism. 89

Why Is Sri Lanka Defying the United Nations?................95

Why Colombo Remains a Challenge for New Delhi.......... 99

Can the Application of Universal Jurisdiction
    Foster Accountability in Sri Lanka?..........................105

Sri Lanka's Chinese Connection: Beyond Bribes and Debts...111

Unsilenced: Male Rape by the Sri Lankan Security Forces....119

Sri Lanka's Tamil Cause, a Political Football ? 124

Sri Lanka's Constitutional Crisis:
    The Geopolitical Dimension......................................129

An evaluation of Sri Lanka's Democratic Credentials 135

How Sri Lanka Wards off War Crimes Investigators 141

The Geopolitics of Sri Lanka's Transitional Justice.........146

Sri Lanka's Muslims Bloodied by Buddhism 152

US Push for New Military Agreement Runs into
    Fierce Opposition in Sri Lanka 158

What Colombo-Beijing Axis Means to Sri Lanka 162

Sri Lanka's Victor's Peace and the Way Forward.............166

(Endnotes).. 173

Acknowledgements

There are four people I like to specially thank for helping me get this book published.

Kulesegaram Sanchayan for his encouragement to have this collection of articles published as a book and Manjula Sri Pathma for designing a cover that graphically captures the main theme underpinning them. I am indebted to Professor Damien Kingsbury of Australia's Deakin University for his foreword identifying the *raison d'être* for these articles written over a ten year period. I thank Associate Professor Jake Lynch, the Winner of the 2017 Luxembourg Peace Prize and Chair of the Department of Peace and Conflict Studies (DPACS) at the University of Sydney for reviewing and commenting on the original draft.

I am indebted to the International Truth and Justice Project (ITJP) for the research undertaken to bring to light many of the war crimes and crimes against humanity committed during the last phase of Sri Lanka's civil war; the ongoing torture of detainees after the war and the Sri Lankan Government's persistent refusal to reveal the fate of those taken into custody. I am equally indebted to the work of the Sri Lanka Campaign, a global non-partisan movement committed to achieving genuine reconciliation based on accountability for violations of international law. I thank these organizations for providing much of the material I have used in writing these articles.

My thanks, not least, to my family, for putting up with me not just for the last ten years but for almost three decades as I took away invaluable family time writing and speaking out about a conflict that had driven over a third of Sri Lanka's Tamils out of the island and had so tragically ended in the imposition of a victor's peace.

Foreword

In 2009, the Sri Lanka armed forces militarily defeated the country's Liberation Tigers of Tamil Eelam (LTTE), with the deaths of some 40,000 civilians in the final few weeks, mostly in what the government called a 'no fire zone'. This event marked the end of a war that had run, in four phases, since 1983. From the perspective of many, perhaps most Tamils, the war was one about not just creating a new, independent state for Sri Lanka's Tamils, but throwing off decades of repression, marginalization and persecution.

The war failed and, as a consequence, the repression, persecution and marginalization has continued apace. Yet the LTTE's struggle and the government's war with it was not just a domestic issue, but involved wider geo-politics and, it might be said, that it was those wider geo-politics that helped bring the war to an end. It is also those wider geo-politics that allow the Sri Lanka government to continue with its policies which, in many respects, have born many of the hallmarks of genocide.

Ana Pararajasingham has long been concerned with the plight of Sri Lanka's Tamils, during the war but especially after, when all that was left were words. His articles in a series of outlets have captured many of the complexities and inter-connected issues that have continued to swirl around the Sri Lanka Tamil issue since 2009. These articles are as alive and as relevant now as when they were published.

As the author notes, events in post-war Sri Lanka have been underpinned by three key themes: Colombo's triumphalist victor's peace; the way in which Beijing's has pursued its ties with Colombo as part of its own wider geo-political strategy, and New Delhi's and Washington's somewhat belated and beleaguered attempts to return themselves to positions of influence in Colombo.

For China, a strategic hold in Sri Lanka places the island state in a prime position in its global Belt and Road strategy to become the world's economic superpower, as well as being a key part of its 'String of Pearls' strategy which locates strategic bases across the Indian and Pacific Oceans. Critically, too, after India's blundered intervention in the Sri Lanka-LTTE war in 1987, China has taken advantage of underlying anti-Indian sentiment and distrust, building a forward base – nominally a port – at Hambantota, just a short distance from China's key regional rival, India.

India has been keenly aware, even alarmed by this shift in regional influence, seeing the regional strategic balance tilted in China's geographic favor, and has sought to rekindle positive relations in Colombo. While this may be too little, too late, it has helped create a situation where China and India compete with each other for Sri Lanka's favors, benefiting the government in Colombo. This has not least been at the expense of the forsaken Tamils who are metaphorically and sometimes literally kicked around as a political football. So, too, the US as a global actor has found itself engaged in Sri Lanka's politics, by way of attempting to thwart its growing global rival, China's influence.

But most importantly, Ana Pararajasingham's articles show that in defeating the LTTE, successive Sri Lanka governments have not wanted to heal past wounds and repair a deeply damaged polity, but have embarked on a triumphalist victor's peace at the expense of building unity and equity.

Sri Lanka's majority Sinhalese Buddhist population has always had a chauvinist nationalist inflection to its political expression but, in the later years of the war and in its peace, this has metastasised to the point where the country's minorities are only suffered as unwanted guests.

Though no longer at war, Sri Lanka's Tamils continue to live at the country's social and political margins in lands still, a decade later, under military occupation.

The author has documented these events and issues in his articles, retaining a clear eye for fact where so many have been persuaded by a regrettable, often confrontational, emotion. For anyone wanting to understand post-LTTE war Sri Lanka, these articles offer invaluable insight. For anyone wanting to understand Sri Lanka's place in the wider geo-strategic field, and to get a glimpse of how global politics can play out in a corner of the world, these articles are enlightening.

I recommend them to you.

Damien Kingsbury
Personal Chair, Professor of International Politics
Deakin University, Australia

Introduction

This book comprises articles of mine published between September 2009 and August 2019 in various journals covering politics and current affairs with a particular focus on Asia and the Pacific. They are commentaries and background pieces as events unfolded in post-war Sri Lanka.

Events in post-war Sri Lanka have been underpinned by three distinct themes: Colombo's pursuit of a victor's peace; Beijing's determination to strengthen the Beijing-Colombo axis and New Delhi's and Washington's attempts to re-assert their influence over Colombo. I have included in this collection two articles on developments in Tamil Nadu as a direct consequence of the happenings in Sri Lanka. The first of these was published in April 2017 by *Open Democracy* under the heading "The Tamil Nadu Factor: Demanding Justice for Genocide in Sri Lanka" and the second, "Is Sri Lanka's Tamil Cause a Political Football?" in *Asia Times* in October 2018. On further reflection, I have included a paper published in *Asia Times* in February 2018 under the heading "*Hindutva* takes on Tamil Nationalism" exploring the contest between the ruling *Bharathiya Janata Party* (BJP) and the state of Tamil Nadu which has resolutely defied BJP's *Hindutva* based nationalism. In view of the strong empathy for the Tamils of Sri Lanka in Tamil Nadu and BJP's desire to gain a foothold in Tamil

Nadu, the situation has the potential to impact New Delhi's Sri Lanka policy and hence its inclusion in this collection. Also included is an opinion piece I wrote for the *Canberra Times* in November 2009 in the context of the refugee flow from Sri Lanka following Colombo's brutal persecution of those suspected to be former Tamil rebels and their families. The piece titled *"Realpolitik Not Humanitarian Concerns Will Decide Myanmar's Future"* draws a parallel between the roles played by international actors in the conflict in Myanmar and Sri Lanka. An article in *Asia Times* in June 2019 titled "Sri Lanka's Muslims Bloodied by Buddhism" attributes the violence unleashed against Sri Lanka's Muslims to triumphalism, the victory over the Tamils having given the Sinhala Buddhist hardliners the impetus to subjugate another non-Sinhala Buddhist group and re-assert Sinhala Buddhist hegemony. The last article in this collection headed "Sri Lanka's Victor's Peace and the Way Forward" appeared on 20 August 2019 in *Daily FT*, an online journal published in Colombo. I chose the *Daily FT* in order to reach out to a Sinhalese readership as the article was based on the premise that the peace that ensues depends on what the victor decides and should Sri Lanka which has pursued a Victor's Peace wish to move beyond it, the responsibility lies with the Sinhalese.

Not surprisingly there is some overlap between articles as they reflect the main themes identified above-the Sri Lankan State's coercive pursuit of a victor's peace and the self interest-driven activities of the US, the global superpower, China, the aspiring superpower and India, the regional power.

I have scrupulously followed the oft-quoted dictum of C P Scott, the legendary editor of *Manchester Guardian* (now the *Guardian), "Comment is free, but facts are sacred"*. All facts have been supported by end notes and articles appear as they were originally published with weblinks replaced by endnotes in respect of those published in online journals.

Although I live in Sydney, a great distance from Sri Lanka, I have closely followed events in that country. I believe distance has given me a perspective that is not readily available for those living close to the happenings.

Ana Pararajasingham
Sydney, Australia
August 2019

South Asia Analysis Group (SAAG)
and also in the Sri Lanka Guardian
9 September 2009

The International Dimensions of the Conflict in Sri Lanka

In May 2009, the three decade long armed rebellion in Sri Lanka ended with the defeat of the Tamil Tiger forces. Beijing provided Colombo not only with military supplies but also diplomatic cover to prosecute the war. China, however, was not the only international actor whose support helped Colombo to vanquish the Tamil Tigers. It was also due to India's logistical support to cut off Tigers' weapons supply. Then there was Pakistan, Sri Lanka's ally of several decades. Iran and Russia had entered the fray invited by Colombo at the behest of China to dilute Indian influence. India's attempt to balance China was driven by the logic that it could not sit back and surrender Sri Lanka into China's embrace. New Delhi wanted to ensure that Colombo stayed within its orbit.[1]

---

1 This was based on a view expressed by Anita Pratap in an article titled "Lessons to be learnt from the rout of the LTTE" –*The Week* 31 May 2009. But since then, others such as Brahma Chelleney have argued that New Delhi was in the dark about Chinese involvement which Sri Lanka had engineered without New Delhi's knowledge. Anita Pratap's article acknowledges that New Delhi's motive in assisting Colombo was also driven by India's goal to be rid of the Liberation Tigers of Tamil Eelam (LTTE).

India

In the early 1980's when Sri Lanka under a pro-western Government began to look to the West in its war against the Tamil rebels, India acted quickly by arming and training the Tamils to exert pressure on Colombo. Consequently, New Delhi was able to persuade Colombo to sign the Indo-Sri Lanka Accord recognizing India's pre-eminence as the regional power. As a result, Colombo remained within India's orbit despite the Northeast of the island coming under the control of the fiercely independent and single-minded Tamil Tigers.

This was largely true until the early years of the 21st century. But, by then the cold war was history and the US-led West had emerged more powerful than ever before. At the same time, the Indian Ocean had become strategically important due to the phenomenal growth of China and India. In this scenario, Sri Lanka due to its location in the Indian Ocean is a strategically significant state.

US and its Allies

Beginning in 2002, the United States had enhanced its involvement in Sri Lanka by backing Norway which had initiated a process to broker peace between the Tamil Tigers and the Sri Lankan Government. The reasons for the 'enhanced' involvement by the US was attributed by US Ambassador Lunstead to the post-Sept. 11, 2001 atmosphere to confront terrorism, the presence of a pro-West Government in Colombo and the personal interest of then-Deputy Secretary of State Richard Armitage. Lunstead identified the first two as enabling factors and the third—the personal involvement of Deputy Secretary Armitage as the one that drove U.S. involvement. Armitage's interest was summed up as one prompted by the desire to help a country torn by conflict, terrorism and human rights abuses. Lunstead was emphatic that this occurred despite the absence of significant U.S. strategic interests in Sri Lanka "contrary to the musings of various South Asian theorists"[1]

But such musings were not confined to South Asian theorists alone, it included others closely involved with the Cease Fire Agreement. Trond Furuhovde, a Norwegian Monitor appointed to oversee the Cease-Fire wrote in the Norwegian Daily, *Adressa* on 30 January 2006 that the role of the Americans was dictated by their new strategy based on their changed interests in Asia. China had increased its presence in these same oceans, as has India. The background for them all is the wish for control of the sea routes from the west, through the Malacca Strait into the South China Sea. In this picture Sri Lanka with its geographic location takes a central place. The east coast of the island with the harbour city of Trincomalee and the Batticaloa lagoon offers extremely important sea-strategic possibilities.

China

But with the election of the stridently anti-Western

Mahinda Rajapaksa as President in 2005, the US and the Norwegians were side lined. China was more than ready to help realizing the tremendous strategic advantage that laid in store should it manage to secure a role for itself as Sri Lanka's main backer. It was successful in this bid. In return, China was permitted to build a port in Sri Lanka's southern coast in Hambantota directly astride the main east-west shipping route across the Indian Ocean. In the process Hambantota became another pearl in China's "String of Pearls" strategy, which has to date involved building ports through the littorals of the Straits of Malacca, Chittagong in Bangladesh; Laem Chabang in Myanmar; Sihanoukville in Thailand and Gwadar in Pakistan. As part of the Hambantota project several thousand Chinese laborers are now in Sri Lanka and Chinese have a visible presence in the island.

In 2009, China provided USD $1.2 billion to Sri Lanka investing in several projects. It is also rebuilding the main roads in the war-shattered Northeast. In 2010, following a three-day visit led by Chinese Vice-Premier Zhang Dejiang to Colombo, as many as six agreements were signed. The agreements cover highways development, enhanced cooperation in information technology and communication, development of maritime ports and the second phase of the Hambontota Port Development Project.[2]

US' Renewed Attempts

The US attempt to bring about a regime change by

backing General Sarath Fonseka, the former army commander and US Green Card holder at the Presidential elections in January 2010 failed when Rajapakse was re-elected President by an overwhelming majority. The US strategy was doomed because of the strong anti-Western sentiments that had come to prevail during the war. These were fuelled by criticism of the Sri Lankan Government's conduct during the final phases of the war by several western governments, media and other agencies. In December 2008, the New York-based Genocide Prevention Project cited Sri Lanka as one of the eight "red alert" countries where genocide and other mass atrocities were underway or risk breaking out. In February 2009, the *Boston Globe* compared the on-going massacre in Sri Lanka to the Bosnian Srebrenica genocide and pointed out that Sri Lanka's armed forces had in the previous month employed indiscriminate bombing and shelling to herd 350,000 Tamil civilians into a government-prescribed "safety zone," where, more than 1,000 were slaughtered and more than 2,500 injured. Several western governments called for investigations into war crimes committed by the Sri Lankan government. The Sri Lankan ambassador to the United Nations in Geneva rejected these allegations as `outrageous` and likened it to asking the triumphant Allies of World War II to be tried for war crimes in the atomic bombing of Hiroshima. Sri Lanka's minister of disaster management and human rights, Mahinda Samarasinghe declared that his government was `sick and tired` of what he called foreign meddling.[3]

It was in this atmosphere that Fonseka announced his candidature for Presidency immediately upon his return from a visit to the US after meeting with officials of US Department of State and Department of Homeland Security. Fonseka was thus seen as a candidate of the West notwithstanding his credentials as a 'war hero' and an ardent ultra-nationalist.[4]

Indian Response to Chinese Presence

Whilst China's overwhelming presence in Sri Lanka is causing some angst amongst Indian political analysts, New Delhi appears to believe that its geographical proximity is sufficient to retain leverage with Sri Lanka. Underpinning this line of thinking is either a confident assumption that it can counter Chinese influence or the notion that it can balance China by assisting in development projects as it assisted during the war.

In a an attempt to retrieve some grounds lost to the Chinese, India has offered to install a 500MW thermal power plant at Trincomalee; construct a rail link between Talaimannar and Madhu; reconstruct the Palaly Airport and re-develop the harbour at Kankesanthurai.[5] Significantly all these projects are in the Northeast of the island- a region overwhelmingly Tamil and referred to as "areas of historical habitation of Sri Lankan Tamil speaking peoples" in the now defunct Indo-Sri Lanka Accord of 1987. Behind India's belated attempt is perhaps the motive to build a strategic presence in a region populated by a people who have been regarded by many an Indian analyst as 'India's natural allies' and thus 'balance' China's influence. This is a weak strategy in the absence of a countervailing force that can contain Colombo.

In any case New Delhi attempts to gain a foothold in the pre-dominantly Tamil Northeast, are undermined by rapid changes to the demography of this region modelled on Chinese actions in Tibet. These attempts can result in a Northeast that is no more Tamil dominated and thus remove the rationale for the strategic space that New Delhi seeks to create. Ramu Manivannan, Associate Professor, with the Department of Politics & Public Administration at the University of Madras in Tamil Nadu has written of historical shifts taking place with profound implications for the future.[6]

Consequently, it is becoming increasingly clear that, the state of Sri Lanka is on its way to be becoming a powerful base from which China contains India on its southern flank, while escalating its incursions into Arunachal Pradesh ('Southern Tibet" in its parlance) from the North. Nor can one discount China's recent deployment of troops into Pakistan -controlled Kashmir which it had provocatively referred to as Northern Pakistan.[7]

Beijing's Aggressive Approach

The West having been forced to forfeit the strategically significant state of Sri Lanka has done little to check Chinese influence in the Indian Ocean. Meanwhile,

Beijing has demonstrated its aggressive trait by deciding to enforce its claim to almost the entire South China Sea as its "historical waters," identifying this as a "core interest" on a par with Taiwan and Tibet.[8] To-date the Obama administration's response to this development has been muted. Earlier, notwithstanding an assessment by Director of National Intelligence Dennis Blair of China as one of the foremost threats to the United States, the administration decided to downgrade China from "Priority 1" status, alongside Iran and North Korea, to "Priority 2".[9] Whilst this has been interpreted as part of the Obama administration's larger effort to develop a more cooperative relationship with Beijing[10], its critics have tended to describe Obama administration's approach as 'appeasement'[11]

While New Delhi seeks to 'balance' and Washington to 'appease', China can only become even more aggressive. in establishing itself as the Asian power. This is in direct contrast to India's position which has been to accept Chinese presence in South Asia as inevitable and accommodate itself to this reality.[12]

It was on Sri Lanka's beach front battlefields that China's "peaceful rise" was completed".[13] Indeed it was in Sri Lanka that China crossed the Rubicon by abandoning its policy of peaceful rise to one of calculated aggression by demonstrating its strategic effectiveness in a region traditionally outside its orbit.[14] More to the point what does this mean in the context of the 'great game' of this century being played out on the waters of the Indian Ocean?

The Canberra Times
11 November 2009

A Safer Place for Tamils

The main cargo of the boat that sank off the Cocos Islands on November 2 comprised 40 Tamil asylum-seekers. Notwithstanding such calamities Tamils will continue to flee Sri Lanka in leaky boats. Many will head to Australia; others to Europe and other parts of the world.

Australia may well grant asylum to these Tamils, that won't stem the flow. But persuading Sri Lanka address the root cause might.

And what is the root cause? The Tamil spokesperson for the refugees put it eloquently when asked if it was fair to jump the queue ahead of other refugees, "I know it's unfair. It's very unfair. But the whole situation is so unfair having no country of your own."

If the Tamils are to stop seeking asylum-their homeland in the north-east will have to be made safe for them. It worked for the Albanians when Kosovo under NATO auspices became independent. It worked in Northern Iraq where a safe -haven was established for the Kurds-in which they exercise self-rule while nominally being part of Iraq. Closer to home, it saved the East Timorese.

In all instances, the West played a crucial role. So why not in Sri Lanka?

Having successfully suppressed the Tamil armed rebellion, Sri Lanka could have resolved the conflict by re-structuring the island into a country of two states (Federal, Associate or Union) maintaining an overarching identity while granting the Tamils what they had fought for the last 60 years (peacefully for the first 30 years and violently thereafter): Self Rule and security.

Instead, it chose to change the demography of the North East in order to deny the Tamils their Homeland. In the process over 300,000 Tamils were incarcerated and several thousands were dispatched to the South. Meanwhile the independent media and the United Nations are kept away as the Tamil Homeland is systematically dismantled.

Australia has a number of avenues open to persuade the Sri Lankan regime evolve a political solution acceptable to all and remove the *reason* for Tamil flight. These measures involve:

- **Calling** for economic sanctions against Sri Lanka and strengthening such measures being considered by European Union countries. The EU, for instance, in an attempt to curb Sri Lanka's human rights abuses is considering withdrawing trade benefits under which Sri Lanka is able to export tax free cheap garments to EU countries.

- **Initiating** actions against senior Sri Lankan Government officials who have a clear case to answer against charges of war crimes. In December 2008, the New York-based Genocide Prevention Project cited Sri Lanka as one of the eight "red alert" countries where genocide and other mass atrocities were underway or risk breaking out. In February 2009, *The Boston Globe* published an article comparing the ongoing massacre in Sri Lanka to the Bosnian Srebrenica genocide. On 18th July this year, the man who commanded the Sri Lankan forces during this onslaught, General Sarath Fonseka, openly admitted to killing unarmed people suspected of being combatants including those "carrying a white flag". On 30th September this year U.S. Secretary of State Hillary Clinton, addressing the UN Security Council, noted that rape has been used as a weapon of war in Sri Lanka.

- **Evoking** the concept known as R2P, or Responsibility to Protect to enable direct intervention to protect the Tamils. "The Responsibility to Protect", is the idea that states have a responsibility to protect their own citizens, but that when they are unwilling or unable to do so, that responsibility must be borne by the broader community of states.

Interestingly one of the most ardent advocates of R2P is Gareth Evans, Australia's former Foreign Minister. It is also likely to be supported by Noam Chomsky who, told a United Nations forum on Responsibility to Protect (R2P), that what happened in Sri Lanka was a major Rwanda-like atrocity, albeit on a different scale. But there was "not enough interest."

Defence Review Asia
March 2011

Sri Lanka: In the Eye of the Storm

When Sri Lanka's brutal civil war ended in 2009 it was noteworthy in several ways-including a rare if not unique example of a Government defeating a long-running insurgency and the related issue of China openly taking sides in a distant internal conflict. In fact it was China's policy-which emerged in full light in 2008-to back the Government in its 25-year struggle with the Liberation Tigers of Tamil Eelam (LTTE) that enabled a victory two years later.

After a US decision to stop selling arms to Sri Lanka in 2007, Beijing quickly stepped into the breach, not only supplying arms and equipment but also invaluable diplomatic support. But this assistance, not surprisingly, has come at a price.

Colombo's decision to boycott the Nobel Prize ceremony in Oslo is as political as the decision by Norway to award the Nobel peace prize to Liu Xiaobo, the Chinese dissident. It was inevitable that Sri Lanka should be drawn into this contest given the crucial role played by China in helping Colombo annihilate the Tamil rebels.

Until this Chinese intervention, Sri Lanka was inexorably tied to the Indian orbit. During the Cold war when India was aligned to the Soviet Union, it ensured that Sri Lanka remained outside the Western camp or for that matter countries India regarded to be inimical to her own interests. In the early 1980's' when a right-leaning Sri Lankan Government attempted to court the West, New Delhi armed and trained Tamil militants to exert pressure on Colombo. Consequently, by 1987, India was able to persuade Colombo to sign the Indo-Sri Lanka Accord acknowledging India's pre-eminence as *the* regional power. As a result Colombo remained within the Indian orbit despite the Northeast of the island coming under the control of the fiercely independent and single-minded Tamil Tigers.

But since the end of the cold war Indian influence has progressively declined. In 2002, the West steadily increased its influence beginning with Norway brokering a Cease-Fire between Colombo and the Tamil rebels. Western involvement was further enhanced when EU, Japan and the US underwrote the peace process and collectively declared themselves to be the co-chairs to the peace process. However, with the election of the stridently anti-Western Rajapakse as President in 2005, the West was sidelined as Sri Lanka moved close to China. China reciprocated by assisting Sri Lanka in its war against the Tamil rebels. India chose to back Colombo in a futile attempt to prevent Colombo coming entirely under Chinese embrace. It was China's unqualified help that ensured this victory.

According Wen Liao[1], a China observer the most remarkable aspect of Sri Lanka's recent victory over the Tamil Tigers was not its overwhelming nature, but the fact that China provided President Mahinda Rajapaksa with both the military supplies and diplomatic cover needed to prosecute the war.

Sri Lanka's increasing closeness to China and its alienation from the West underpin a serious shift in the emerging new world order where China regards itself as *the* power to counter the US-led west. It no longer subscribes to its earlier model of 'peaceful rise'. Indeed, it has been argued that it was' on Sri Lanka's beachfront battlefields, that China's "peaceful rise" ended giving way to a more assertive China.

An assertive China is a cause for concern not only to the US but also to other international powers-notably India. This concern is compounded by the fact that China now has untrammeled access to the most strategic location in the Indian Ocean-the island of Sri Lanka. There is growing consensus that during the twenty-first century as the Indian Ocean emerges to be the centre stage, US, China and India will compete for control and influence. India cannot help but be wary of the growing capability of China's navy and Beijing's growing maritime presence. Then there is the strategy known as a 'string of pearls' which has involved China building bases in Myanmar, Bangladesh, Pakistan and Sri Lanka encircling India in the process. In Sri Lanka, the port at Hambantota sits directly astride the main east-west shipping route across the Indian Ocean denying India the advantage it had hitherto taken for granted.

Given this scenario, it comes as no surprise that India and the US should seek to align themselves. More than an inkling that such an alliance was in the making was foreshadowed when Robert Blake[2], Assistant Secretary, of US State Department announced on 30th September 2010 that India was the United States' "indispensable" partner for the 21st century and was of "strategic importance to the United States". Earlier under Secretary of State, William Burns had announced that India and America now mattered more to one another During President Obama's visit to India in November, the Indian Prime Minister and the US President reaffirmed this position by describing the India-US. Strategic partnership to be indispensable not only for their two countries but also for global stability.

Sri Lanka's Chinese connection places it in the eye of the storm as India and the West seek to re-assert their influence in the Indian Ocean.

Frances Harrisons' *Still Counting the Dead*

Tales from a War without Witnesses

The book provides an illuminating account of the final five months of the battle between Sri Lanka's military and the Tamil Tigers based on accounts provided by survivors in a war without witnesses. It is pointed out that the absence of witnesses was an important part of the Sri Lankan Government's strategy as aid workers and international journalists were ordered out of the war zone.

The harrowing details of the final days are told through multiple voices focusing on the experience of individuals under chapters titled: The Journalist, The Spokesperson, The Doctor, The Nun, The Teacher, The Rebel Mother, The Volunteer, The Fighter, The Shopkeeper and The wife.

It opens with an aid worker accusing the Sri Lankan Government of slaughter after expelling the UN from the war zone. The tales narrated by the traumatized survivors makes it clear that the slaughter of the civilians was not just collateral but a deliberate part of a wider strategy. Tamil civilians appear to have soon realized that they were being lured into safe zones (mostly hospitals) only to be targeted. Included is a `private' account provided to Harrison by a UN official confirming that the government had declared safe zones only to gather civilians in one place to kill as many as possible. Harrison calls it a slaughter on "an apocalyptic scale".

Harrison is hard on the Tamil Tigers who in the last desperate days had begun forced conscription and restraining civilians from leaving. And these were civilians who had retreated along with the Tigers until defeat had become obvious.

The book also deals with treatment of the survivors after the Tamil Tigers were vanquished. The case of Manimoli ("The Wife") who was subject to multiple rapes by Sri Lankan Policemen prompts Harrison to suggest that rape of Tamil women in custody continues with impunity and that it was generally understood in the Tamil community that Tamil women in custody were often raped. Harrison cites an observation by senator Hillary Clinton, US Secretary of State in late 2009 that Sri Lanka was a country where rape had been used a tactic of war and raises the matter of Sri Lankan officials using Tamil women from refugee camps to running prostitution rackets. She refers to Sri Lanka's Defence Secretary making light of rape by pointing to an attractive British Tamil woman who had not been raped. The fate of female combatants held in captivity is questioned and attention drawn to the extraordinary fact (in comparison to other conflicts) that there have never been any allegations of rape leveled against the Tamil rebels. The latter is attributed to the Tamil Tigers' avowed feminist ideology.

Harrison admits she cannot prove every single detail of the accounts given to her. She points out that the patterns of the stories match each other and support the findings of a UN advisory Panel (In 2011, a UN Advisory Panel found there was credible evidence of war crimes in the last stages of the conflict).

Still Counting the Dead is confined to the narratives of the survivors. It quite deliberately avoids the politics that underpinned the violence unleashed against the Tamils. This is not necessarily a shortcoming as this apparent omission is likely compel the intelligent and the interested to seek a deeper understanding of the conflict that was brought to an end only through the massacre of tens of thousands of Tamils by the Sri Lankan state.

The book is a necessary read for anyone who seeks an understanding of the horrendous manner in which the Sri Lankan Government ended the war.

Required: A Sri Lanka Policy[1]

In December 2004, I wrote a paper titled "India's Sri Lanka Policy: Need for A Review" (first published in the website of the South Asian Analysis Group) arguing that that there was a need for New Delhi to review its Sri Lanka Policy.

My argument was based on the premise that a country's national interests are served only when policies are based on ground realities. I pointed out that India's Sri Lanka policy did not reflect ground realities, which, at that time meant acknowledging the existence of two distinct power centres in Sri Lanka-Colombo in the South and Killinocchchi in the North. The implication was clear-New Delhi should seek to improve its leverage by adopting a more nuanced approach to ensure that its own interests were not compromised.

Instead, New Delhi, dictated by the belief that by helping Colombo reassert its dominance over the entire island it could keep Sri Lanka within its orbit provided Colombo with logistical support to cut off Tigers' weapons supply. It did not foresee Colombo counterbalancing Indian influence by bringing in China. Even after China's direct involvement, New Delhi continued to extend its support to Colombo driven by the logic that it could not sit back and surrender Sri Lanka into China's embrace.[2] In the meantime, by making New Delhi complicit in the brutal manner in which it brought the war to an end, Colombo has more than counterbalanced Indian influence. New Delhi's apparent complicity in the horrendous war crimes committed during the final stages of the war has compromised New Delhi's capacity to influence Colombo. New Delhi's impotence is not only due to its suspected complicity but also because of the demise of the Liberation Tigers of Tamil Eelam (LTTE). As the International Crisis Group pointed out "With the LTTE gone, the Indian government may have lost its best opportunity to influence Sri Lankan policy... That powerful leverage has now been lost".[3]

What New Delhi had not quite thought through in implementing its policy which was primarily focused on getting rid of the LTTE[4] can be broadly summarised as follows:

(a) *A complete failure to grasp the agenda of the Sri Lankan State in respect of the Tamil people in Sri Lanka.*

The Sri Lankan State given its unitary constitution is a state where all political power resides with the majority Sinhala nation. This is because within the confines of a unitary state the Sinhalese who make up well over seventy-five per cent of the population are a permanent majority. Since its independence in 1948, this Sinhala dominated state has relentlessly pursued an agenda of completely Sinhalising the state. This agenda is informed by the ideology that the entire island belongs only to the Sinhalese and the Tamils are interlopers. This is a well understood ideology explored in depth by several academics, Sinhalese, Tamils and those from the international community. It is this notion which has driven successive Sri Lankan governments to pursue Sinhalisation through various means and thereby deny the Tamils a distinct identity as a people occupying a contiguous well defined area-the Tamil Homeland. Consequently any arrangement that provides autonomy to the Tamils is anathema to the Sinhala dominated Sri Lankan state. Hence, Mohan Ram's conclusion in *Sri Lanka the Fractured Island* that the " Sinhala majority has all along thought that any Tamil demand can only be met the cost of its own interest, a zero sum game... and is not reconciled to even providing limited concessions the Tamils were given under the Indo Sri Lanka Agreement"[5]

New Delhi appears to have not grasped this basic tenet underpinning the actions of the Sri Lankan state. Its hope that with the demise of the LTTE, Sri Lanka could be persuaded to at least 'devolve' some political power to the Tamils was entirely misplaced. New Delhi's role in cooperating with Colombo appears to have been predicated by the flawed perception that once the LTTE is liquidated the Sinhalese could be persuaded to provide concessions to the Tamils.

Instead, the Sri Lankan state has taken advantage of the military solution which it had imposed with New Delhi's help to further its own agenda of Sinhalising the state through changing the demography of the Tamil Homeland. This is being pursued through a strategy of 'Ethnic flooding'[6] whereby the Tamil Homeland is flooded with Sinhalese population, initially, with families of the armed forces and thereafter with civilian settlers. New Delhi has been completely outsmarted by this strategy which has the potential to render any 'devolution' meaningless.

(b) *A failure to evaluate the impact of China's direct involvement in Sri Lanka*

It has been argued that India's involvement in Sri Lanka has been underpinned by the doctrine that Colombo should remain exclusively within New Delhi's sphere of influence. This is based on the premise of India being the regional power and Sri Lanka, a state within this region.[7] By permitting China's entry, New Delhi has in effect not only abandoned this policy but appears to have endangered its own geopolitical interests.

(c) *A failure to realise the impact in Tamil Nadu*

New Delhi has failed to factor into its strategy of assisting Sri Lanka, the fall out in Tamil Nadu. The manner in which the victory was achieved through the deployment of genocidal violence and the role played by New Delhi in extending its support to the Sri Lankan regime has alienated Tamil Nadu. Sam Rajappa, writing for the *New Statesman* noted that Tamil Nadu is on the boil due to India's contribution to the genocide (of Tamils) in Sri Lanka and should Rajapaksa and company are hauled up before the International Court of Justice at The Hague, New Delhi cannot escape responsibility for this horrendous brutality.[8] In 2011, Tamil Nadu Assembly adopted a unanimous resolution seeking the imposition of economic sanctions against Sri Lanka by India. The resolution moved by Chief Minister Jayalalitha also wanted India to press the United Nations to declare as "war criminals" those who committed crimes during the conflict in Sri Lanka.[9] New Delhi's impotence or unwillingness to press for a strongly wondered resolution at the March 2013 UNHCR sessions has made it untenable for the Dravida Munnetra Kazhagam (DMK) the ruling party's ally in the Central government to continue its support for a government that is widely viewed by Tamil Nadu as having betrayed the Tamil people. In March 2013, the DMK withdrew its support greatly undermining the Congress led UPA's capacity to stay in power.

It is imperative on the part of New Delhi's policy makers to review the failed Sri Lanka policy and forge a bold approach to regain some influence in the region.

This bold approach must primarily address the on-going plight of the Tamil people in Sri Lanka taking into account the agenda of the Sri Lankan state and its inclination to continue with the zero sum game. As part of its Sri Lanka policy New Delhi can and indeed should seek to protect the Tamil people by transforming the Tamil homeland in Sri Lanka into a protectorate. There is precedence for such an act in the protection that the US was able to provide for Iraq's Kurdish population in northern Iraq.

If New Delhi is able to successfully implement such a policy it can serve its interest in many ways. Apart from addressing the Tamil Nadu factor, it can also provide New Delhi the strategic space to counter the increasing Chinese influence in Sri Lanka. Such a policy will also be in keeping with the advice proffered by Professor Sumantra Bose[10] in 2007 in the course of his key note address at a seminar[11] exploring the international dimensions of the conflict in Sri Lanka. According to Bose, despite the unhappy history of the last twenty years, it is with the Tamil people of Sri Lanka that India needs to build its alliance. New Delhi ought to build on the natural affinity between India and the Tamil people of Sri Lanka. There is no other community that has such powerful affinity of a historical and cultural nature with India. He made this point in the context of the perception by the Indian establishment "with good cause" that it is surrounded by hostility in the region.[12]

The Diplomat
December 30 2015

Colombo's Military Build-Up:
A Strategy of Deterrence

What might explain the recent increase in defense spending?

Contrary to expectations that with the end of the civil war, Sri Lanka would reduce its spending on defence, Colombo has in fact increased its defence expenditure. Defence spending in 2009, the year the civil war ended with the comprehensive defeat of the Tamil Tigers, was Rs 175 billion ($1.2 billion). By 2011, this had risen to Rs 194 billion, and in 2013 it was Rs 235 billion. In late 2015, Colombo was looking to procure 18 to 24 new fighter aircraft to replace its obsolete fleet of MIG-21s by 2017.[1] The budget allocation for defence in 2016 is Rs 307 billion.

Colombo's 2009 victory over the Liberation Tigers of Tamil Eelam (LTTE) was achieved with heavy civilian casualties. Tens of thousands were killed and maimed. There was a purpose, to convince the survivors of the heavy price of war and remove the risk of any future uprising. Colombo was successful and knows it. Not only have thousands of Tamil Tiger soldiers been killed, but many thousands of former fighters and other young men and women have fled the country in fear of their lives. Thousands of others[2] are believed to be in government custody. Another uprising is highly unlikely.

Why then should Colombo spend a significant proportion of its GDP on defense, funds that could otherwise be spent on restoring the country's war-ravaged economy? What exactly is the rationale for this exponential increase in defense spending?

If internal threats are non-existent, the threat must be external. From Colombo's perspective, the major threat has always been its giant neighbour, India. It is a fear that has plagued Colombo since the late 1940s when Sri Lanka was about to be granted independence following Britain's decision to relinquish India, the Jewel in the Crown. In 1947, Sri Lanka's first Prime Minister, D. S. Senanayake, based the strategy of his country's security on the assumption that the most likely threat to its independence would come from India. The British saw in these perceived fears a strategic advantage, linking the granting of independence to the island under a unitary constitution that gave the Sinhala majority enormous political power, while defense agreements gave Britain the use of naval and air bases in Trincomalee. The base in Trincomalee was of strategic significance to Britain, especially for securing links to Australia and New Zealand. D. S. Senanayake considered the unitary constitution as a safeguard against the Tamils federating with India, just as Ulster separated from the Irish Republic to federate with Britain, another of his fears and one that he shared with Lord Soulbury, the head of the commission appointed by the British to draft a constitution for the island.

Until the early 1980s, New Delhi sought to allay Sri Lanka's fears through displays of generosity in bilateral relations. These included accepting in 1964 over half a million Tamils of Indian origin who had been disenfranchised by the Sri Lankan government in 1948; maintaining a cordial relationship with Sri Lanka despite the latter's pro-Pakistan position during the Indo-Pakistani War of 1971; and conceding the disputed island of Kachatheevu to Sri Lanka in 1974.

By the early 1980s, however, India's actions appeared to justify Sri Lanka's suspicions when it armed and trained Tamil militants to exert pressure on Sri Lanka, which was showing clear signs of moving into the Western camp. These suspicions were only reinforced when India intervened directly in 1987 under the Indo-Sri Lanka Accord to deny the use of the Trincomalee Harbour to the U.S. and the setting up of a Voice of America broadcasting facility in Sri Lanka.

Although India provided Colombo with training and logistical support during Colombo's final assault on the Tamil Tigers, this did not allay Colombo's reservations about India. Colombo knows that New Delhi's assistance to defeat the Tamil Tigers was to eliminate the organization that had assassinated Rajiv Gandhi, and was being made at the behest of Rajiv's widow Sonia, who pledged full military support to Sri Lanka to achieve that goal.[3]

Although Colombo's war efforts had the support of New Delhi, it balanced that relationship by maintaining strong relationships with China and Pakistan. Without the help of the Chinese, who, in addition to their military aid, gave the Sri Lankan government diplomatic cover[4] at the UN Security Council, Colombo could not have won the long-running civil war. Subsequently, when Colombo's relationship with China grew stronger under President Mahinda Rajapaksa, Washington and New Delhi played a crucial role in bringing about a new government in Colombo. Sri Lanka's new leader is decidedly pro-Western, but like all its predecessors, the new government has its reservations about New Delhi. A Crisis Group report in 2011 noted that with the LTTE gone,[5] New Delhi's capacity to influence Sri Lankan policy has been greatly reduced. Yet still Colombo mistrusts New Delhi. To many Sinhalese, India's overt intervention in 1987, citing the plight of Tamils was a humiliating affair. At that time Sri Lanka's armed forces were a fraction of their current strength, and were barely capable of dealing with the Tamil insurgency underway.

And so the victory over its internal foe, achieved with Chinese assistance, has provided Colombo with an opportunity to build up its forces as a deterrent against any future actions by what many Sinhalese perceive to be their external foe: India.

South Asia Journal
16 January 2017

Sri Lanka's Re-embrace of China Leaves India out in the Cold

Beijing lost much of its influence over Sri Lanka following a regime change in early 2015 that saw pro-Beijing President Mahinda Rajapaksa ousted. The new government promised a 'balanced approach' to dealing with the major powers-Washington, the global superpower, Beijing, the aspiring superpower and India, the regional hegemon. However, within two years Colombo has renewed its special relationship with Beijing by agreeing in late 2016 to buy military transport airplanes from China and give 80 per cent of the Hambantota deep seaport on a 99-year lease to China for US$1.1 billion,[1] not to mention the offer to renew the Chinese-funded Colombo Port Project suspended in the wake of the 'regime change'.

The regime change failed because its architects, Washington and New Delhi had underestimated Beijing's resolve. Beijing's direct intervention in Sri Lanka's civil war was a game changer that marked China's end of 'peaceful rise'[2] and its replacement by an assertive policy underpinned by an agenda to expand China's options while limiting those of potential adversaries. Beijing's direct intervention in Sri Lanka's long running civil war was a game changer which held consequences for Washington and New Delhi.

Not that Washington or New Delhi was unaware of the consequences. In December 2009, the US Senate Foreign Relations Committee noted Sri Lanka's strategic drift (towards) China to have consequences for U.S interests called for increasing US leverage vis-à-vis Sri Lanka by adopting a robust approach to secure US interests.[3]

The 'robust approach' involved the US supporting the United Nations Human Rights Commission (UNHRC) resolutions between 2011 and 2014 calling for investigations into war crimes committed during the latter stages of Sri Lanka's civil war. The 2014 resolution called for the UNHCR to undertake a 'comprehensive investigation into alleged serious violations and abuses of human rights and related crime'.[4] The purpose was two-fold: one to exert international pressure on the Colombo government and the other to convince the Tamil voters that a new regime would punish those responsible for the war crimes and thus gain their crucial support to oust Rajapaksa. Faced with the growing intimacy between Beijing and Colombo, New Delhi joined Washington.

Washington rewarded the new government by postponing the March 2015 UNHRC hearings on Sri Lanka's war crimes and just prior to these hearings in September 2015, reversing its call for an international investigation. In December 2015, Washington declared Sri Lanka to be a country that promotes the values of democratic governance and respect for human rights, freedom of navigation, sustainable development and environmental stewardship.[5] Washington's readiness to abandon the 'stick' and use the 'carrot' seems premature. But with a West-leaning Prime Minister and Foreign Minister in the Colombo Government, Washington may well believe it has secured a foothold in Sri Lanka and a carrot was necessary.

At the beginning, New Delhi was hamstrung in supporting the UNHRC resolutions having supported Colombo's campaign against the Tamil rebels. However, faced with the growing intimacy between Beijing and Colombo, New Delhi showed no hesitation in help bring about a regime change working in tandem with Washington. In early April 2016, Sri Lanka's Prime Minister Wickramasinghe, in announcing the renewal of the Chinese funded Colombo Port City Project declared that the cooperation between China and Sri Lanka would intensify and go far beyond that[6]. In the same month, Colombo flatly denied the claim by India's Road Minister Nitin Gadkari of discussions[7] on constructing a bridge connecting the two countries. When Indian soldiers were killed in Kashmir, New Delhi expected other SAARC (South Asian Association for Regional Cooperation) members to condemn it as a Pakistan sponsored terrorist act and withdraw from the SAARC summit to be hosted by Pakistan. Afghanistan, Bangladesh and Bhutan promptly withdrew. Sri Lanka offered condolences to families of the victims but did not withdraw. Instead, Sri Lanka's Foreign Minister told the Sri Lankan parliament 'There was no question of pulling out when there was no summit to attend'.[8]

Colombo's swift turn around vis-à-vis New Delhi is not surprising. Colombo has always countered its giant neighbour's influence by forging close relationships with those opposed to it. During the Indo-Pakistani war in 1971, Colombo supported Pakistan by providing re-fuelling facilities. During the cold war, Colombo maintained a pro-Western policy in contrast to New Delhi which had a special relationship with the Soviet Union. Little wonder the rationale for the 'regime change' was questioned within days on the grounds that given the geopolitical underpinnings of the Beijing-Colombo axis it was unlikely that Colombo's relationship with China would drastically change merely because one president is replaced by another.[9]

Realizing Colombo was fast slipping away; New Delhi invited President Sirisena for bilateral talks[10] in mid-October. Later, the Indian Foreign Secretary met with the Sri Lankan President in Colombo,[11] followed by another visit to New Delhi by Sirisena on 6 November.

Alerted by this flurry of visits, in early November, the Chinese Ambassador to Sri Lanka chastised Sri Lanka for its lack of consistency in implementing the Colombo Port Project and warned Sri Lanka faces the risk of losing foreign direct investments if it fails to maintain a consistent policy.[12] Colombo capitulated by agreeing to buy planes from China and lease the Hambantota port to China.

New Delhi faces considerable difficulties given Colombo's historical antipathy and Beijing's proactive stance. In the words of one of India's renowned political writers, Brahma Chelleney, New Delhi is also constrained because "Indian diplomacy still lacks teeth".[13]

Open Democracy
13 April 2017

The Tamil Nadu Factor: Demanding Justice for Genocide in Sri Lanka

Just prior to the United Nations Humans Rights Council's (UNHCR) March 2017 hearings on war crimes committed during Sri Lanka's civil war, the main political party of Sri Lanka's Tamils, the Tamil National Alliance (TNA), had urged the UN to pressure the Sri Lankan government to expedite its investigations. Instead, the consensus resolution passed on 23 March provided the Sri Lankan government with a further two years to investigate the war crimes. This comes as no surprise because the March 2017 resolution, like all previous resolutions on war crimes committed during Sri Lanka's civil war, was initiated and backed by the US.

Between 2012 and 2014, the US-backed resolutions in the UN were designed to pressure Sri Lanka, which, under the presidency of Rajapaksa, had become a close ally of Beijing. However, following the regime change that saw Rajapaksa ousted and Wickramasinghe, from the right-leaning United National Party (UNP), appointed Prime Minister, the US changed tack.

Thereafter, the resolutions were intended to maintain US influence by placating Sri Lanka's Sinhala political establishment, which was opposed to the very notion of war crimes.

Ever since Tamil Nadu became aware of New Delhi's assistance to Colombo during the final days of Sri Lanka's civil war, it has been on the boil.

New Delhi, which had worked in tandem with the US in ousting the pro-Beijing Rajapaksa, had gone along with the consensus resolution of March 2017, but found it necessary to explain its stance. India's external affairs minister Sushma Swaraj, justifying her government's role in supporting the March 2017 resolution, told the Indian upper house, the Rajya Sabha, that India's approach in the UN Human Rights Council was guided by the premise that the protection of human rights can be best pursued through constructive and collaborative engagement, and that its aim is to "protect the interests of Tamils in Sri Lanka".[1]

New Delhi's compulsion to explain its position is directly attributable to what can be best described as the "Tamil Nadu Factor". Two days prior to the passing of the resolution which allowed Sri Lanka a further two years to investigate the alleged war crimes, a demand was made in the Rajya Sabha by Vasudevan Maitreyan[2] from Tamil Nadu's ruling party, the All India Anna Dravida Munetra Kazhkam (AIADMK), that India should oppose the resolution. Vaiyapuri "Vaiko"

Gopalsamy, an Indian politician from Tamil Nadu, described a clause in the resolution, which required foreign jurists, lawyers and rapporteurs investigating alleged war crimes to obtain Colombo's consent, as the 'unkindest cut'.[3]

The ruling party in New Delhi, the Bharatiya Janata Party (BJP), has reasons to be concerned with Tamil Nadu's sentiments, given that Tamil Nadu is on the cusp of change[4] following the untimely demise of its charismatic chief minister Jayaram Jayalalithaa. Ever since Tamil Nadu became aware of New Delhi's assistance to Colombo during the final days of Sri Lanka's civil war, under a congress-led coalition, it has been "on the boil".[5] The initial protests in January 2009 involved self-immolations, galvanizing over a hundred thousand people to take to the streets. The protests were led by students from colleges across the state. Although the state government was able to eventually quell the unrest, much of the anger remained. The first political casualty of the suppressed anger was the Dravida Munnetra Kazhagam (DMK), the ruling party in the state, which was in alliance with the Congress party in the central government during New Delhi's assistance to Colombo. At the state elections in May 2011, two years after the decimation of the LTTE, DMK was comprehensively defeated by its rival the AIADMK, which had taken advantage of the suppressed anger.

In June 2011, the Tamil Nadu Assembly, now dominated by the AIADMK, adopted a unanimous resolution seeking imposition of economic sanctions against Sri Lanka. In March 2013, following another state-wide protest by students focusing on war crimes committed against Sri Lanka's Tamils, the state assembly passed another resolution calling for the establishment of a separate state for the Tamils of Sri Lanka. The AIADMK's stance paid off at the 2014 general elections, helping it secure 37 of the 39 seats. Although the BJP had swept the polls in most other states, it could secure just one seat in Tamil Nadu. In 2015, faced with the prospect of a UN resolution against Sri Lanka's war crimes being confined to a domestic investigation instead of the international investigation that had been demanded by Sri Lanka's Tamils, the AIADMK-led Tamil Nadu Assembly passed yet another resolution calling on New Delhi to support an international probe against those who had committed war crimes. The 2016 state elections vindicated AIADMK's stance, helping it beat its rival and defying the trend in Tamil Nadu since 1984 of the voting out of the incumbent party.

The protest was the product of Tamil Nadu's anger at the Indian political establishment for its support of what is perceived by Tamils an act of genocide.

Beginning mid-January this year, the state of Tamil Nadu was the scene of a seven-day-long non-violent protest which ended in violence when police intervened on the eighth day. The protests began, innocuously enough, as a demonstration against the banning of *jallikattu,* an ancient sport involving the taming of a raging bull. It soon morphed, however, into a state-wide movement attracting tens of thousands voicing concerns over a range of issues. Seemingly over multiple issues, the protest was in fact the product of Tamil Nadu's suppressed anger at the Indian political establishment for its support to what is largely perceived by Tamils the world over as an act of genocide. This perception was not groundless. In December 2008, the New York-based Genocide Prevention Project had identified Sri Lanka as one of the eight "red alert" countries where genocide and other mass atrocities were underway, and in February 2009, the Boston Globe compared the atrocities taking place to the Bosnian Srebrenica genocide[6]. Then there was the finding by former BBC Correspondent in Sri Lanka, Francis Harrison, that the government had declared safe zones during the latter stages of the war only to gather civilians in one place to kill as many as possible.

Since 2009, all protests—including the last protest in January 2017—were led by students. Should the next leader emerge from the generation that had spear-headed protests forcing the AIADMK to pass resolutions in support of the Tamils of Sri Lanka, the Tamil Nadu Factor may prove to be decisive in shaping New Delhi's Sri Lanka policy.

4 August 2017
South Asia Journal

Extension Given to Probe Sri Lanka's War Crimes is No Surprise

In late March this year, the United Nations Humans Right Council (UNHRC) granted Colombo a further extension of two years to probe alleged war crimes committed during the civil war. The main political party of Sri Lanka's Tamils, the Tamil National Alliance (TNA), went along with this decision because it meant Sri Lanka would continue to be under international supervision for a further period.

Sri Lanka's Tamil people are understandably disappointed. So are the people of the Southern Indian state of Tamil Nadu, home to over seventy million Tamils. Two days prior to the resolution being passed allowing Sri Lanka an extension of two years, a demand was made by V Maiteryan from Tamil Nadu's ruling party, the All India Anna Dravida Munetra Kazhkam (AIADMK) in the *Rajya Sabha* that India oppose the resolution. Instead, New Delhi supported the resolution.

The extension comes as no surprise given the rationale behind UNHRC resolutions on Sri Lanka since 2012. The primary motive for the US backed resolutions in the UNHRC since 2012 was to increase US leverage vis-à-vis Sri Lanka and stem Sri Lanka's drift towards China under the Rajapaksa Presidency. Indeed, as early as December 2009, the US Senate Foreign Relations Committee report, "Sri Lanka: Re-charting US Strategy after the War" had noted that Sri Lanka's strategic drift (towards) China will have consequences for U.S. interests in the region and had called for adopting a multifaceted, broader and more robust approach to secure US interests. In view of the substantial evidence pointing to war crimes that implicated Rajapaksa, the US was well equipped to pressure the Sri Lankan Government. The US backed resolutions between 2012 and 2014 calling for war crimes to be investigated by a body of international experts was part of this robust approach. Rajapaksa, though unsettled by these resolutions was emboldened by Beijing's continued support.

In January 2015, Rajapaksa was ousted and replaced by his former colleague Sirisena who appointed Ranil Wickramasinghe from the right-leaning United National Party (UNP) and the preferred candidate from Washington's point of view as Prime Minister in the new 'unity Government'. The regime change was directly attributable to US' continued pursuit of the robust approach. In this case it involved working in tandem with New Delhi which had become uneasy with Colombo's provocative stance of taking on a decidedly pro-Beijing position ignoring New Delhi's attempts to court Colombo. Matters came to a head when Colombo's provocative posturing involved permitting

Chinese submarines to dock in Colombo during 2014 and brushing aside New Delhi's concerns.

Having wielded the 'stick' to unsettle Rajapaksa, the US was quick to employ the 'carrot' to consolidate the new regime. Thus the March 2015 hearings of the UNHCR to consider progress made by Sri Lanka to investigate the war crimes was postponed to September 2015, a move initiated by the US, now an ally of the new regime. Although, there was some opposition from the EU countries on the grounds that the postponement may result in a precedence, the US stance prevailed. The US continued to wield the carrot during the September 2015 proceedings by amending the March 2014 resolution calling for an international investigations into a domestic accountability mechanism with international involvement. In effect, a hybrid mechanism that was a far cry from the international investigations envisaged earlier. The US intention to down grade the accountability process was made evident in late October 2015, when US Assistant Secretary of State Nisha Biswal called for a collaborative resolution.[1] Notwithstanding these developments, a senior member of the Tamil National Alliance (TNA), M A Sumanthiran told this writer in early November 2015 that he was confident of the resolutions being implemented as agreed in view of Britain's continued support. The extension granted in March 2017 suggests this confidence to be misplaced. In April 2016 Samantha Power, U.S. permanent representative to the United Nations, in an attempt to further reassure Colombo, made an extraordinary statement claiming that Sri Lanka has, since January 2015, emerged as a global champion of human rights and democratic accountability.[2]

The US backed resolutions in the UN on Sri Lanka's war crimes passed between 2012 and 2114 were designed to pressure the Rajapaksa regime which had become a close ally of Beijing. Thereafter, the resolutions were intended to maintain US influence by placating Sri Lanka's Sinhala establishment which is opposed to the very idea of war crimes. The Sri Lankan President Sirisena's flat denial of allegations of' war crimes in an interview with Al Jazeera's Hoda Abdel-Hamid,[3] in January 2016 and former President Chandrika Kumaratunga ruling out the involvement of courts[4] to probe war crimes in February 2017 are products of this mindset.

The two year extension granted to implement the earlier resolutions is patently part of the strategy to keep the Sinhala political establishment onside.

The Politics of Persuasion-An Evaluation

Politics is about power. Power is about people.
James Margach, The Anatomy of Power (1979)

Although, it is just over eight years since the armed conflict between the Sri Lankan state and the Liberation Tigers of Tamil Eelam (LTTE) was brought to an end, the root cause that gave rise to the brutal war remains unresolved. Nor has been there any progress in addressing the consequences of the armed conflict. Significant parts of the Tamil homeland are under army occupation; an investigation to identify the perpetrators of war crimes is yet to commence and Tamil political prisoners continue to languish in jails where torture is routine[1]. Meanwhile, the spectre of 'disappearances' haunt the Tamil people as former LTTE fighters and those suspected to have had links to the organisation are systemically hunted down.

Background

Not surprisingly, the demise of the LTTE resulted in Tamil leadership coming to reside with the Tamil National Alliance (TNA), which, since its inception in

2001[2], had worked in tandem with the LTTE. In the wake of the LTTE's defeat, the TNA adopted what has been described as a 'pragmatic approach' to deal with the Sri Lankan Government by basing its demand on the premise that the Government is likely to concede 'little' rather than more.[3] The party therefore sought to frame its demand within the concept of shared sovereignty coupled with a gradualist approach to improve on its initial demands. These demands were based on the 13th amendment to the Sri Lankan constitution introduced under the Indo-Sri Lankan Accord of 1987. As this amendment included a clause that called for certain powers to be devolved to a single entity dominated by Tamil speakers, it required the merger of the Tamil dominated Northern and Eastern Provinces into a single unit-the Northeast Province. However, in 2006, this particular clause was deemed *ultra vires* by the Sri Lankan Supreme Court which ordered that the Northeast Province be demerged into a Northern and Eastern Province.

More to the point, the 13th amendment is inherently incapable of devolving any real power to the Provincial Council because it contains a provision that ensures ultimate political power resides not with the Chief Minister or the Provincial Councillors but with the Governor of the Province-an appointee of the President. The role of the Chief Minister is limited 'to 'aid and advice' the Provincial Governor in the exercise of his functions. Hence, the characterisation of the 13th amendment as 'a constitutional sleight of hand.[4]

Other inadequacies of the 13th amendment stem from several subjects being kept out of even the Provincial Governor's powers, let alone the Provincial Council.

Well aware of the limitations of the 13th amendment, the TNA sought to rely on the goodwill of the Sri Lankan state, India and the US-led-West to realise its goals by improving on the 13th amendment. Presumably, these included addressing the matter of political power being exercised by Colombo via the Governor and expanding the subjects coming under the purview of the Provincial Council.

In early 2010, some members of the TNA broke away from the party arguing that the party was not being true to its ideals and had forfeited its principles. The breakaway group called itself the Tamil National People's Front (TNPF) and rejected the 13th amendment as a starting point for any negotiations. The terminology used by the TNA and TNPF were similar, they both emphasised self-determination. However, the TNPF did not compromise on earlier positions taken by Tamil political parties within the confines of the sixth amendment to the Sri Lankan constitution precluding Tamil independence. TNPF's demand therefore was for a new constitution on the basis that Sri Lanka comprises two nations. More importantly, TNPF subscribed to the view that since the Tamil people's struggle for self-determination had been exploited by the international actors (the US-led West, India and China) to further their own interests, Sri Lanka's Tamils should take advantage of this to secure a truly federalist constitution.[5] In an interview, the leader of the TNPF, Gajendrakumar Ponnambalam, went on to expand on this theme by suggesting that the Tamil people need to formulate a foreign policy of their own to deal with the international actors.[6]

Not surprisingly, the international actors (India and the West) found TNA's stand helpful because it made it easier for them to manage Colombo, their primary objective. Although TNPF's grasp of the international dimensions underpinning the conflict was accurate, the party was ineffective in communicating its policies.

TNA was helped by the widely held notion that it was an LTTE proxy. Then there were those who found TNA's pragmatic approach to their liking and that of the TNPF too theoretical and too confronting. The TNA also had the advantage in building its profile among the people because *Uthayan*, the most popular daily in the North was owned and managed by one of its own parliamentarians. Many believed that by breaking away from the TNA, the TNPF had weakened the Tamil polity.

Consequently, it was the TNA that emerged as the main political party of Sri Lanka's Tamils.

The Politics of Persuasion

The primary approach of the TNA was informed by the twin assumptions that it was necessary to allay

Sinhala fears of Tamil separatism and Tamils had little countervailing power to bargain with the Sinhala leadership. Then there was the belief that Washington with its 'Liberal Peace Agenda' and New Delhi with whom TNA's leader Rajavaraothayam Sampanthan enjoyed a 'special relationship' would help persuade Colombo agree to a meaningful power-sharing arrangement with the Tamil people. Driven by this belief, the TNA threw its support behind the New Delhi and Washington orchestrated 'regime change' to dislodge Rajapaksa. Once the new regime came into existence, the TNA in pursuit of its cooperative approach participated in Sri Lanka's independence celebrations on 4 February 2015. It was the first time since 1972 that a party representing the Tamil people of the Northeast had participated in such an event. Party leader Sampanthan explained the reason for the participation as one designed to

> 'send a signal to the Sri Lankan people and the country to seek their constructive support to resolve the problems of the Tamil people and their participation was an indication of their reposing of trust in the leaders of the new government of a commitment to address the problems of the Tamil people in the right spirit.'[7]

TNA's next step was to ask the Tamil people permit TNA handle negotiations with the Government and not rock the boat.[8] This particular request did not go down well with the ordinary people who demanded that the party spell out its position openly. Then there was the need to counter the TNPF, whose demands were in line with the aspirations of the common people. To make matters even more difficult, the Chief Minister of the Northern Provincial Council, a TNA appointee, Wigneswaran, appeared to support the views of the TNPF while distancing himself from any direct dealings with the TNPF. Faced with the general elections in August 2015, TNA upped the ante.

On 15 May 2015, during a televised debate with the TNPF's Gajendrakumar Ponnambalam, TNA's Mathiyaparanam Sumanthiran, revealed that the TNA had an 'understanding' with the Sri Lankan President to provide the Tamils with a measure of autonomy 'outside the unitary constitution amounting to federalism in substance'. In July 2015, TNA announced that a new constitution was needed to address the 'Tamil question'[9]. TNA's election manifesto emphasised self-determination, the merger of the Northern and Eastern provinces and power sharing arrangements based on a federal structure. Addressing the media in Jaffna, Sumanthiran articulated that the TNA's manifesto had gone beyond the *Thimpu* principles[10] to accommodate the Oslo Declaration (a joint declaration by the LTTE and the Sri Lankan Government in December 2002 agreeing to explore a solution on the principle of internal self-determination within a united Sri Lanka).[11] TNA's election campaign was well received because by reiterating its commitment to 'Thimpu Principles' and its readiness to embrace the 'Oslo Declarations', it left no doubts about its commitment to a truly federal resolution to the conflict. There was more than a hint during TNA's campaign that a new constitution was indeed in the offing. Unsurprisingly, in the pre-dominantly Tamil Northeast, the TNA swept the polls with 16 seats. Its election strategy was, no doubt, a resounding success.

TNA's hope for a new constitution addressing Tamil concerns appeared to be on track when the Sri Lankan Parliament, on 9 March 2016, agreed to transform Parliament into a Constitutional Assembly with the power to draft a new Constitution. But by end of 2016, it was clear that Colombo's political establishment had lost its enthusiasm for a new constitution. In November 2016, TNA's Sumanthiran, frustrated by these developments and the government's reluctance to move beyond the 13th amendment, announced that the TNA's conciliatory approach should not be taken as 'a sign of weaknesses.[12] This was ironical because TNA's entire approach from the very beginning was based on a perception of weakness - a party devoid of any countervailing power. It is argued that it was this perception of weakness that prevented TNA from factoring into its approach strategies to counter the all too common practice of the ruling Sinhala party blaming Sinhala opposition to back down on its promises to the Tamil people. Instead, TNA relied on a conciliatory approach and the belief that the international community would intervene to persuade Colombo resolve its longstanding conflict with the Tamil people.

Is this assumption by the TNA of the Tamils as a people completely devoid of countervailing power, accurate? In the wake of the LTTE's crushing defeat, the victorious Rajapaksa Government was not one to seek political accommodation with the Tamil people. Instead, the approach was to further militarise the Tamil region. In 2013, $US 2.2 billion was allocated towards defence expenditure, a twenty-six per cent increase from 2012.[13] The purpose was to saturate the Tamil Homeland with a large military presence and keep the population subjugated. As a consequence, the ratio of all military and paramilitary personnel to civilians rose to be close to the 1:5 ratio.[14]

Rajapaksa regime, particularly after its victory over the Tamil Tigers was marked by a complete absence of the rule of law. Arbitrary arrests and 'disappearances' were common, intimidation of political opponents was routine. The army was engaged in a well-orchestrated campaign to terrorise the Tamil population into submission. It was during this period that thousands of young Tamils fled the country seeking asylum in Europe, Australia and neighbouring India. In 2012, of the 17,000 people who arrived by boats seeking asylum in Australia, 6,500 were from Sri Lanka.[15] Indeed, many of these young Tamils left the island from ports under the control of the Sri Lankan navy aided and abetted by the Sri Lankan authorities determined to ethnically cleanse the Tamil region.

In this environment, TNA's inclination to assume that

the Tamil people had little voice and no countervailing power to bargain is understandable. It therefore relied on the US-led campaign to exploit war crimes committed during the latter stages of the war to exert pressure on Rajapaksa believing this might either cause Rajapaksa to seek accommodation with the Tamil people or bring about a regime change that would result in a government more likely to address the Tamil question. Washington's primary motive to bring about a regime change was driven by Sri Lanka's strategic drift towards China that held consequences for the U.S.

Similarly, New Delhi was perturbed by Colombo's clear preference for Beijing over New Delhi. Both New Delhi and Washington were dictated by self-interests in bringing about a regime change. Tamil support was crucial to bring about a new regime. TNA obliged, but did little to take advantage of the situation to extract promises from the global powers (Washington and New Delhi) to **publicly** commit their support for self-rule for the Tamil homeland. It is argued that such a step would have helped TNA build its countervailing power in the form of international recognition of Tamil right to self-determination, albeit 'internal'. TNA clearly missed out on this opportunity.

The TNA also missed out on the opportunity to build its countervailing power immediately following the regime change in early 2015. On the immediate term, the change of government resulted in an easing of the oppressive conditions that had prevailed under the previous regime. TNA had the opportunity during this period to mobilise mass support around self-rule, return of lands occupied by the army and the disappearances of young Tamils suspected to have had links with the Tamil Tigers. History teaches us that mass mobilisation can cause governments, especially those who are under the close scrutiny of international bodies to heed their voices. Such a mobilisation might have even found support amongst the liberal Sinhalese, but more importantly it had the potential to cause neighbouring Tamil Nadu take a more proactive stance in taking up the issue.

It is argued that the TNA, dependent on New Delhi's 'good offices', purposely refrained from mass mobilisation because it was not in New Delhi's interest to have Tamil Nadu take up the issue. New Delhi is understandably averse to its domestic politics influencing its foreign policy. It explains the Northern Provincial Council's Chief Minister Wigneswaran's behaviour during the early days when he was very much part of the triumvirate comprising Sampanthan, Sumanthiran and himself. In September 2013, Wigneswaran, chided Tamil Nadu politicians for intervening in Sri Lanka's 'internal' affairs which he compared to a home where the husband and wife are having a fight and went on to say: "We will fight, but sometimes we come together. The next door neighbour must not come and say 'you must divorce, you must divorce'. That is not your business."[16] No doubt, at that point Wigneswaran shared the belief that relying on the good will of New Delhi was the way to obtain concessions from Colombo.

However, Wigneswaran's actions since then have gone some way in building the countervailing power of the Tamil people through mass mobilisation. This has to date involved passing a resolution in the Northern Provincial Council identifying the Sri Lankan state as a perpetrator of genocide, initiating events like *'Eluga Thamil'*, joining in the commemoration of the Mulivaikal massacre and openly articulating the Tamil cause. Wigneswaran's transformation is attributable to his move to the North as its Chief Minister and his exposure to ground realities. Wigneswaran's actions since then can be understood as an attempt to tap into the strong sentiments of the people to build a countervailing force.

Unfortunately, TNA's approach of relying on the good will of the Sri Lankan political establishment and the international actors alone while **eschewing direct engagement** with the Tamil people has not helped the party.

With the benefit of hindsight, it can be argued that TNA has become a prisoner of its own approach proving the Tamil truism *'Mudhal Konal, Mutrum Konal'(If crooked at first, it will be so throughout).*[17] However, such an argument would imply that the entire approach of the TNA was flawed. This is not the case. TNA's attempt to allay Sinhala fears by **not** adopting a confrontationist position is a positive attribute in view of the party's pursuit of a negotiated political resolution. TNA can become stronger by engaging strategically with the international actors and mobilising the people around its political agenda as spelt out in its 2015 election manifesto.

The Diplomat
9 September 2017

Sri Lanka: Sovereignty Compromised

Colombo's attempt to balance India and China has proved futile.

Addressing the Indian Ocean Conference in Colombo on August 31 this year, Sri Lankan Prime Minister Ranil Wickramasinghe was confident that Sri Lanka is poised to become the "Hub in the Indian Ocean.[1]" That was not all, with air and sea connectivity it was only a matter of time for Sri Lanka to emerge as a centre for offshore finance, a competitive manufacturer, and service provider. The prime minister's assessment was made in the context of the island's strategic location in the Indian Ocean, its two international airports and several ports dotting its 1,340 kilometre coastline.

It was a promising picture.

While Colombo does possess several ports and two international airports, the control of major ports and the second international airport located in Matalla is severely undermined by the involvement of China and India. The rationale for the involvement of these two Asian giants in the operation of Sri Lanka's ports is not economic but strategic. Therein lies Sri Lanka's predicament: It has little control over all its ports.

The management of Hambantota port is no longer under the direct control of the Sri Lankan state. Its operation is controlled by China via its state-owned company, China Merchants Ports Holdings. Beijing, having "invested" around $1.6 billion in building the port, reaped the benefits when Colombo was unable to make repayments on the "loan" and was thus forced to sell a 70 percent stake to the China Merchants Ports Holdings, which is to operate the port over a 99-year lease. The formal agreement was signed on July 31.

Then there is the white elephant, Matalla's International Airport, dubbed "The World's Emptiest International Airport[2]" is also located in the Hambantota district. The airport was built at a cost of $209 million of which $190 million was in the form of loans from China. The airport was unable to generate any business because of its remote location out in the jungles of southern Sri Lanka devoid of infrastructure or even much of a resident population. In August 2017, India offered to purchase a 70 percent stake in the dysfunctional airport over a 40-year lease It was an offer very similar to the one that saw Hambantota port come under Chinese management. Obviously, India's offer was not driven by economic goals given the airport's remote location. But, coming as it did within weeks of Sri Lanka's agreement to grant control over the Hambantota Port to the Chinese, there are good grounds to regard the offer as an Indian initiative to counter the growing Chinese presence in southern Sri Lanka. Colombo is reportedly viewing the Indian offer separately[3] from the other seven proposals (including a proposal from China), implying that New Delhi is being assertive in its quest for the port.

India has a presence in the northern Sri Lankan port of Kankesanthurai (KKS) where it has been involved since June 2011[4] mapping, as well as removing and disposing vessels sunk during the civil war. However, India's primary interest lies in controlling the eastern Port of Trincomalee. In early February 2017, India made this clear during a Carnegie (India)-hosted event in Colombo titled "Trincomalee Consultations.[5]" In late April, when New Delhi invited the Sri Lankan prime minister on a five-day visit to India, the Indian Ministry of External Affairs, in announcing the visit emphasized that discussions would take place around operating a major oil-storage facility and a Liquefied Natural Gas (LNG) plant in Trincomalee in addition to developing the port of Trincomalee as a key transit point.[6] In May, when the Indian Prime Minister paid his second visit in two years to Sri Lanka, it was reported that India would take up the issue of China's growing influence in the island with Sri Lanka[7]. New Delhi could not have made its intentions more clear.

China's interest in Sri Lanka's ports is said to be driven by its "One Belt, One Road" project establishing new trade routes linking China with the West by road and sea. India, however, is inclined to view Chinese presence in Sri Lanka in terms of the "String of Pearls" theory implying that Beijing's interest is driven by its goal to encircle India. As such India looks upon Chinese presence as a threat and is therefore likely to continue exerting pressure on Colombo for a greater role and an enduring presence.

Neither of the powers is likely to give up on their goal of bringing Colombo within their own sphere of influence. China has the wherewithal in terms of financial resources and has considerable support amongst Sri Lanka's political establishment suspicious of India's expansionist intentions. New Delhi counts on its geographical proximity, U.S. support ,and exploiting Tamil grievances to arrogate a role for itself. Colombo's attempt to balance by playing these powers against each other has proved futile. Instead, Colombo's sovereignty has been greatly compromised as it is forced to serve two masters.

Defence Review Asia
September -October 2017

Trincomalee Beckons: Is New Delhi Becoming Assertive?

India and Sri Lanka have always had a complex relationship. New Delhi's frustration with Colombo is the latter's reluctance to accept India as *the* regional power. Instead, Colombo has always looked to other powers to counter Indian influence. During the Indo-Pakistani war in 1971, Colombo supported Pakistan by providing re-fuelling facilities. During the cold war, Colombo maintained a pro-Western policy when a right wing government was in power and a strictly non-aligned stance when under a socialist regime. Colombo stayed away from the Soviet Union mainly because New Delhi had forged a special relationship with the Soviet Union during this period. In recent times, Beijing took advantage of Colombo's antipathy to New Delhi to gain a foothold in Sri Lanka.

The regime change in January 2015 backed by New Delhi and Washington, designed to dislodge Beijing did not help India to the extent it benefited the US. The Prime Minister in the new 'Unity' Government' headed by President Sirisena is Ranil Wickramasinghe, the leader of the West leaning United National Party(UNP), a majority in the Sri Lankan parliament. Thanks to the UNP, the

US has some clout with Colombo. At the same time, the UNP, along with the rest of Sri Lanka's political establishment find New Delhi problematic. Beijing has exploited the Colombo- New Delhi divide and its own financial hold on Sri Lanka to compel Sri Lanka re-embrace China. As a result, today, China has a significant presence in Sri Lanka, an island of considerable strategic significance in the Indian Ocean. One of India's renowned political writers, Brahma Chelleney, believes New Delhi is constrained because "Indian diplomacy still lacks teeth".[1]

Recent events, however, suggest that New Delhi is beginning to show some teeth in stemming Colombo's return to Beijing. On Tuesday, 4 April, speaking in Colombo at the launch of Sri Lankan Prime Minister Ranil Wickcramasinghe's biography[2], Sashi Tharoor, former Indian diplomat and currently the Chairman of the Indian Parliamentary Standing Committee on External Affairs could not have been more direct. Having pointedly referred to China's ambitions in the South China Sea extending well into the Indian Ocean, Tharoor went onto say that "India and Sri Lanka need to look to a future in which our geographical proximity becomes a reason for closeness rather than controversy". Later, raising the 'string of pearls' theory that sought to explain China's inclination to build maritime infrastructure along the Indian Ocean periphery, including one in Sri Lanka, Tharoor told the audience "what we offer is not the roar of a super power, but certainly something better than being one among several jewels – pearls or otherwise – in another country's geopolitical calculations". Tharoor's not-so-subtle message was simple and straightforward -it's best that Colombo stays within the Indian orbit. The message was all the more significant as it was delivered to an audience that included Sri Lanka's President Maithiripala Sirisena, Prime Minister Ranil Wickramasinghe and several high ranking Sri Lankan politicians.

Earlier in February this year, Carnegie India hosted its first conference outside India in Colombo[3]. Participants included senior government officials and scholars from Bangladesh, India, Japan, Maldives, Nepal, Norway and Sri Lanka. China was a notable absentee. More to the point, the Conference dubbed 'Trincomalee Consultations,' was all about Trincomalee, home to the world's second largest natural harbour located on Sri Lanka's north-eastern coast. Matters discussed centred around the geostrategic significance of the Indian Ocean; about the continuing importance of Trincomalee in terms of its strategic significance; the need to improve its connectivity; the development of Trincomalee harbour as a 'Regional Hub' and Trincomalee harbour's role in reintegrating the region. The conference was framed as a track 1.5 dialogue implying that it involved informal participation by decision makers and state representatives. There are good reasons to regard 'Trincomalee consultations' hosted by Carnegie India, as an Indian initiative. Not only because the Indian Government was represented by a high ranking Indian official, the Joint Secretary (Policy Planning) from the Ministry of External Affairs (MEA) , but mainly because of the subject matter-Trincomalee. Trincomalee's importance to New Delhi cannot be understated. The primary reason for India's direct intervention in Sri Lanka's internal conflict since the 1980's was the perception that the Sri Lankan Government was prepared to grant the US rights for military facilities including the use of the Trincomalee harbour. And, central to the Indo- Sri Lanka Accord signed between the Sri Lankan President and the Indian Prime Minister in July 1987 was the clause: "Trincomalee or any other ports in Sri Lanka will not be made available for military use by any country in a manner prejudicial to India's interests". From India's point of view this remains true to this day. Participation by India in the Carnegie-India hosted 'Trincomalee Consultations' underscores this point.

In announcing Sri Lankan Prime Minster Ranil Wickaramasinghe's five day visit to India beginning 25 April, officials from the Indian Ministry of External Affairs said that discussions would take place around operating a major oil-storage facility and a Liquefied Natural Gas (LNG) plant in Trincomalee in addition to developing the port of Trincomalee as a key transit point.[4] More to the point, the hastily arranged meeting came just a few weeks before Wickcramasinghe's planned trip to attend the Belt and Road Summit in Beijing. The Indian diplomatic initiative also involves a trip by the Indian Prime Minister Narendra Modi to Sri

Lanka in May this year, the second visit in two years. According to Indian Newspapers, it is expected that India will take up the issue of China's growing influence in the island with Sri Lanka[5].

Taken together, the diplomatic initiative of Carnegie India, Tharoor's tough message, Wickramasinghe's visit to India to be followed by the Indian Prime Minister's visit to Sri Lanka, it is hard to refute that New Delhi has begun to adopt a more robust approach in dealing with its recalcitrant neighbour.

Realpolitik Not Humanitarian Concerns Will Decide Myanmar's Future

In a brief opinion piece for *Asia Times*[1] published on 4 October 2017, I argued that the persecuted Rohingya's fate will be decided not by humanitarian concerns but by geo-politics. This was despite the United Nations and Human Rights Watch agreeing that the violence amounted to "textbook example of ethnic cleansing"[2]

I also argued, as the violence unleashed by the Myanmar authorities against the Rohingya is underpinned by the intent to eradicate their identity as a distinct ethnic group, it meets the UN's Genocide Convention. And in this situation, international law demands direct and immediate intervention.

In this article, I propose to show that at the end of the day it will be the self-interests of international actors that will prevail deciding the fate not only of the victims, the persecuted Rohingya, but also that of the perpetrator, the Myanmar state. This is the nature of *realpolitik* which is entirely devoid of moral or ethical considerations.

A good example of the potency of *realpolitik* in shaping the lives of people persecuted by the state giving rise to armed uprising is that of Sri Lanka's Tamils. Targeted by the Sri Lankan state-orchestrated pogroms since the 1950's, the Tamils embarked on a violent campaign against the state in the late 1970's. The state responded by unleashing the worst pogrom of all in July 1983. The scale of the violence was such that within just two weeks over 3,000 Tamils were murdered; properties destroyed and tens of thousands were forced to flee to the Northeast of the island-the Tamil Homeland. The intensity of the violence gave rise to it being dubbed 'Black July'. International outcry followed. The International Commission of Jurists (ICJ) declared the violence to be "a series of deliberate acts, executed in accordance with a concerted plan, conceived and organised well in advance"[3] and concluded that these actions "amounted to acts of genocide"[4]. Canada opened its doors on humanitarian grounds to all Tamils fleeing the violence. Australia was more circumspect by permitting just those Tamils who had families to sponsor their migration under a Special Humanitarian Program (SHP). The definition of 'families', under SHP was extended to include those well beyond one's own immediate family permitting many survivors to escape the violence. The actions of Canada, Australia and several European countries in this instance were driven by humanitarian concerns. However, as the conflict intensified, geo-politics became the main driver with US, China and India vying to bring Colombo under their respective spheres of influence. As a consequence,

Sri Lanka's Tamils paid a huge price in terms of death, destruction and dispossession.

The Sri Lankan state, the perpetrator of these atrocities did not get away either. Sri Lanka's much vaunted sovereignty has been severely compromised as international actors have intervened directly bringing about regime changes and taking control over several ports. Today, the management of Hambantota port is no longer under the direct control of the Sri Lankan state. Its operation is controlled by China via its state-owned company, China Merchants Ports Holdings. India has a presence in the northern Sri Lankan port of Kankesanthurai (KKS) where it has been involved since June 2011 mapping, as well as removing and disposing vessels sunk during the civil war.[5] Furthermore, India has made its intentions clear that its primary interest lies in controlling the eastern Port of Trincomalee and in this regard has taken several measures to bring Colombo in line. Meanwhile, the US is in a position to influence Colombo thanks to Ranil Wickramasinghe , the right-leaning Prime Minister of the country.

In the case of Sri Lanka and Myanmar's 'political Buddhism' played a crucial role in the attacks mounted against the Tamils and the Rohingya. And in both cases the violence worsened after the persecuted decided to strike back. Violence against the Tamils intensified when the Liberation Tigers of Tamil Eelam (LTTE) ambushed and killed 13 army men in July 1983 and against the Rohingya after the Arakan Rohingya Salvation Army

(ARSA) attacked 30 police posts in one night killing several policemen. The more telling comparison will be when the various international actors begin to respond in pursuit of their own vested interests.

The posturing by India, China and the US has begun in earnest. India, mindful of developing access to ASEAN markets and countering Chinese dominance in Myanmar has taken a decidedly pro-Myanmar stance by strongly condemning the 'terrorist attacks on Myanmar security forces'[6]. China which competes with the US for influence in Myanmar, has endorsed Myanmar's offensive against Rohingya Muslim insurgents.[7] Washington, while expressing concern about the violence has stopped short of criticizing the country's government or its de facto leader, Nobel laureate Aung San Suu Kyi.[8] Aung San Suu Kyi's 'western credentials' explain Washington's disinclination to condemn Suu Kyi. Suu Kyi can prove to be a useful ally in countering China's influence. Then there is the 'Islamic' threat that looms large as experts[9] warn of Islamic State (ISIS) recruiting fighters from the Rohingya.

Regional and global powers will not want to distance themselves from Myanmar, however, repugnant its treatment of the Rohingya. Instead, attempts will be made to demonise the Rohingya to justify the actions that geo-politics demand. The recent well publicized news of the Rohingya Muslims turning on the Hindu Rohingya based on photos released by the Myanmar Government is perhaps the beginning of this process.

It is only a matter of time for geopolitics to outweigh any humanatrian concerns. The internationalisation of the conflict is bound to shape Myanmar's future. A Reuter report indicating that China is seriously pushing Myanmar to give it an 85 percent stake in a strategically important sea port at Kyaukphyu[10] point to yet another parallel between these two countries.

Asia Times
25 October 2017

Sri Lankan Constitution: The Strategy of Doublespeak

It is hard to refute the assertion that the conflict in Sri Lanka between the Sinhala-dominated state and the Tamil people is directly attributable to the unitary constitution under which the island was granted its independence by Britain in 1948. Unitary constitutions crafted on the principle of "one person, one vote" results in political power residing mainly with the majority nation to the detriment of the numerically smaller nations in a multinational state.

Faced with disenfranchisement, discrimination and denial of fundamental rights, the beleaguered Tamil leadership demanded a federal constitution, widely regarded as an antidote to the "tyranny of the majority." When this was denied and periodic pogroms were unleashed to beat the Tamils into submission, they escalated their demand by calling for independence. The "civil war" that resulted in the wake of this demand lasted well over a quarter of a century. It ended with the defeat of the Tamil rebels in 2009. The brutal war has left the Tamils and Sinhalese even more polarized, but the untrammelled majoritarian rule that was the root cause is yet to be honestly addressed.

The interim report released by the Steering Committee of the Constitutional Assembly on September 21 has been criticized for suggesting a form of government calling for "maximum devolution" and avoiding the term unitary in the Tamil and English versions of the interim report. The critics are strong adherents to the existing unitary form of government.

The Sinhalese version of the interim report explicitly states that the constitution will be *aekiya rajyaya* (unitary in Sinhalese), consistent with all previous constitutions enacted since 1948. Unlike the previous constitutions, the interim report on the new constitution does not explicitly refer to "unitary" in the Tamil and English versions. Instead, the terms used are *orumiththa nadu* in Tamil, which means united, and "indivisible" in English. The term "federal" has been studiously avoided in all versions of the interim report. In Prime Minister Ranil Wickremesinghe's own words, this was because the people in the south (Sinhalese) are fearful of the word "federal" and people in the north (Tamils) are fearful of the word "unitary."

The devil being in the detail, should the constitution be challenged, it will be the original Sinhala version that will prevail. As such there are good reasons for the Tamil people to question the validity of the proposed constitution. Had the government headed by Wickramasinghe and President Maithiripala Sirisena been serious about finding an enduring resolution of the 70-year-old conflict, efforts should have been directed at allaying Sinhala fears, not in crafting a disingenuous report to deceive the Tamils.

The Sinhala fear of a federal form of government is driven by two distinct notions:

- The belief that a "federal" constitution would pave the way for the Tamil northeast to secede.

- The assumption that the presence of 70 million Tamils in Tamil Nadu can cause India, the regional power, to intervene in a Cyprus-type partition of the island once a Tamil-speaking federal unit is established.

Both notions have been arduously promoted by fear mongers pursuing their own political agenda.

If the Sirisena-Wickramasinghe administration was serious about resolving the conflict and since it can only be resolved through a federal constitution, the concept of federalism within the confines of a single country should have been explained long before the interim report was released. No such action was undertaken. Nor have attempts been made to allay Sinhalese fears about New Delhi's foreign policy being influenced by Tamil Nadu, causing India, the regional power, to undertake a Cyprus-type partition of the island. New Delhi's foreign policy in respect of Sri Lanka is all about ensuring that the entire island stays within its sphere of influence and not breaking up the island. Even while arming Tamil rebels who were fighting to establish an independent Tamil state, India was clear in its objective. Jyotindra

Nath Dixit, the Indian ambassador to Sri Lanka (1985-89), made it plain in his book *Assignment Colombo* that breaking up Sri Lanka would make it difficult for India to maintain its own territorial integrity in the face of separatist demands in Punjab and Kashmir. Then there was MJ Akbar, an influential member of the Indian political establishment and currently the national spokesperson for India's ruling *Bharatiya Janta Party*, who, in an article titled "Why we are in Sri Lanka" in February 1988, wrote:

> A new flag anywhere in the world is a dangerous thing; it breeds new ideas. One has no doubt that the first requirement for India at this sensitive moment in our history is to be very clear in both our minds and in our policies that we will not support any secession anywhere, not in our country, not in our neighborhood.

It is not that fear mongers in Sri Lanka are unaware of New Delhi's foreign policy, but it serves their political agenda to engage in these tactics to tap into a mindset that over the years has been groomed to look upon New Delhi with great suspicion.

In July this year, Sirisena emphasized[1] that no change will be made to the clauses of the Constitution regarding the unitary status of the country. The declaration was made to the Buddhist Chief Sanganayaka. Wickramasinghe was equally clear when he declared in September that under the proposed constitution Sri

Lanka will remain a unitary state with priority given to Buddhism.[2] It is clear that the prime minister and the president are determined to continue with the unitary *aekiya rajyaya* constitution while appearing to promote devolution.

It is a strategy best described as doublespeak.

The Diplomat
12 November 2017

Sri Lanka's Proposed Constitution Comes Under Attack

International interest, not international laws, will deliver autonomy to Sri Lanka's Tamils.

The interim report on Sri Lanka's proposed constitution released on September 21 has come under a spate of attacks. On October 24, a retired Sri Lankan army officer, Major General Kamal Gunaratne, insisted that those seeking to introduce the new constitution are traitors who must be killed. Four days earlier, Dayan Jayatilleka, a former diplomat, had called for rising up and confronting the prime minister,[2] whom he identified as one of the architects of the interim proposals and in early October, a Sri Lankan academic, Asoka Bandarage, challenged the government's legitimacy to change the constitution. Meanwhile, the all-powerful Buddhist clergy has firmly vetoed the proposals on the grounds that it would undermine Sri Lanka's unitary governance.

The opponents to the proposed constitution are incensed by the term "maximum devolution" used in the proposal, because it envisages devolving power to the Tamil-dominated Northern and Eastern Provinces.

That the other seven Sinhala-dominated provinces will also be recipients of devolved power does not enter the argument; after all, the existing, highly centralized unitary constitution already vests power with the Sinhala people. Although it is widely recognized that it was the island's unitary constitutions (enacted in 1948, 1972, and 1978), which ensured all political power resides with the numerically larger Sinhala people, were the root cause of the 26-year civil war, political power-sharing remains anathema to a significant section of the Sinhala political establishment.

The opposition to devolving political power to the Tamil-dominated Northern and Eastern provinces is driven by two well-ingrained notions. The first is the fear that increasing autonomy could pave the way for Tamils to secede. Second is the long-held belief that the island of Sri Lanka is a designated sanctuary for Theravada Buddhism, the purest form of Buddhism, and as such precludes political power sharing with non-Buddhists. This phenomenon is identified as "Political Buddhism."

In actuality, any question of the Tamil-dominated northeast region seceding has been comprehensively addressed in the interim report, which categorically states that the country will remain an "indivisible united" entity. To make the position even more clear, the official Sinhala version of the interim proposal uses the word *ēkīya* (unitary in Sinhalese) to describe the constitution, while studiously avoiding the word unitary and federal in the English and Tamil versions. While this may well address the fear of secession, the mindset shaped by Political Buddhism remains a significant obstacle to enacting the proposed constitution.

Well aware of this hurdle, on October 30, Tamil parliamentarian MA Sumanthiran made a moving case for a political power sharing arrangement and concluded by pleading with every member of the Assembly[3] to support the change. Such pleas were common in the Sri Lankan parliament during the first 30 years of its existence and were persistently ignored by the Sinhala polity, which enjoyed unrestrained political power under the unitary constitution. On two occasions, agreements reached with the Tamil leadership for a limited degree of autonomy were abandoned in the face of opposition no different than what is being voiced now. And it is likely that this plea too would fall on deaf ears. The scenario unfolding is eerily familiar, a classic case of "back to the future." It is as if the civil war that tore the island apart had never happened!

Meanwhile, the chief minister of the Tamil–dominated Northern Province, CV Wigneswaran, convinced that Sinhala leadership is unlikely to willingly share political power, has argued that Sri Lanka's Tamils should try to obtain their rights by resorting to international laws.[4] *Realpolitik,* however, tells us that it is not international law but international actors pursuing their own interests that dictates international intervention. Should Wigneswaran be able to factor into his argument that an autonomous northeast could help counter Beijing's growing influence over Colombo, he may well succeed in winning international support for self-rule for Tamils within a united country.

The Diplomat
25 November 2017

India's Regional Power Credentials under Threat by China

In both Maldives and Sri Lanka, China has been chipping away at Indian influence.

Maldives is the smallest nation in South Asia in terms of population, area and GDP. Yet in August 2017, it defied India, the regional power, by permitting three Chinese warships to dock in Male. The Beijing-Male axis began when Chinese President Xi Jinping visited Male in September 2014, during which Beijing secured Maldives' agreement to become part of China's Maritime Belt and Road Initiative, much to New Delhi's consternation.

In return, Beijing made large investments in infrastructure projects in Maldives, including the China-Maldives Friendship Bridge between the airport located in Hulhumale and Male. When Maldives cancelled its agreement with the Indian company, GMR Male International Airport Limited (GMIAL), to modernize and operate its international airport for 25 years, GMIAL took the case to an international arbitral tribunal, which ordered that GMIAL be paid $270 million in compensation. This was paid promptly by the

Maldives government, but India suspects China put up the amount.[1]

More worrying for India is China's presence on Maldives' northernmost atoll, sitting in the middle of the busiest transit point between the Middle East and Southeast Asia.[2] By extending loans to Maldives to build its infrastructure, China has the island state over a barrel. According to former Maldivian President Mohamed Nasheed, 70 percent of Maldives' foreign debt is owed to China, on which the loan interest alone "is more than 20 percent of Maldives' budget.[3]"

China's approach in bringing Maldives into its orbit is in many ways reminiscent of its approach in bringing Sri Lanka into its sphere of influence.

In Sri Lanka, by backing Colombo in the civil war prosecuted by then-Sri Lankan President Mahinda Rajapaksa, China gained considerable influence over Colombo. Without Chinese backing, Rajapaksa's government would have had neither the wherewithal nor the will to ignore world opinion in its offensive[4] that decimated the Tamil Tigers, the Tamil rebel army that had been known officially as the Liberation Tigers of Tamil Eelam (LTTE), along with tens of thousands of civilians. Rajapaksa in turn began to align Colombo with Beijing, much to the discomfort of India, which regarded itself as the regional power. The Sri Lanka-Maldives relationship also strengthened under the pro-Beijing Rajapaksa's rule, during which period the

Chinese president visited Colombo and Male.

The new administration in January 2015, backed by New Delhi and Washington with the intent of dislodging Beijing, did not help India to the extent it benefited the United States. This is because, the prime minister in the new "unity" government' headed by President Maithripala Sirisena is Ranil Wickramasinghe, the leader of the Western-leaning United National Party (UNP). At the same time, the UNP, along with the rest of Sri Lanka's political establishment, finds New Delhi problematic. Beijing has exploited the Colombo-New Delhi divide and used its predatory pricing methods to compel Sri Lanka to re-embrace China. As a result, today, China has a significant presence in Sri Lanka, an island of considerable strategic significance in the Indian Ocean. This includes the right to operate the Hambantota port through a 99-year lease.

New Delhi has been less than vigilant in permitting Beijing a role in what it has always regarded as its own backyard. Sri Lanka is just 32 kilometers from India's southern coast and the Maldives 717 kilometer away.

It was New Delhi's readiness to help Colombo in its war against the Tamil rebels that gave Colombo the diplomatic space to enable Beijing's involvement in Sri Lanka. New Delhi allowed this to happen because it had under estimated Sri Lanka's diplomatic skills and was blind to Beijing's global ambitions. India's loss of leverage with Colombo following China's intervention in Sri Lanka's civil war was noted by the International Crisis Group, which observed,[5] "With the LTTE gone, the Indian government may have lost its best opportunity to influence Sri Lankan policy. That powerful leverage has now been lost."

As Indian analyst Brahma Chellaney[6] noted:

Sri Lanka, for its part, practiced adroit but duplicitous diplomacy: It assured India it would approach other arms suppliers only if New Delhi couldn't provide a particular weapon system it needed. Yet it quietly began buying arms from China and Pakistan without even letting India know. In doing so, Colombo mocked Indian appeals that it rely for its legitimate defence needs on India, the main regional power. It was only by turning to India's adversaries for weapons, training and other aid that Colombo pulled off a startling military triumph.

In the wake of Colombo's victory over the Tamil rebels , China observer Wen Liao noted perceptively in an article aptly titled "China Crosses the Rubicon[7]" that for two decades China was guided by the concept of "peaceful rise," but that concept in reality ended on Sri Lanka's beachfront battlefields. In the 1990s, China sought to hide its "peaceful rise" behind a policy of "smile diplomacy" to allay its neighbours' fears. In pursuit of this trade barriers were lowered, while soft loans and investments were extended to its southern neighbours.

Today, China seeks to shape the diplomatic agenda in order to increase its options while constricting those of potential adversaries. Indeed, Beijing's presence in Maldives is part of this strategy.

New Delhi has only itself to blame for letting Colombo and Male moving away from its sphere of influence.

Asia Times
5 December 2017

Sri Lankan Regime Backing Away from Conflict Resolution Vows

In contrast to promises it made before coming to power, the Sri Lankan government of President Maithripala Sirisena has recently taken a tougher, pro-Sinhala nationalist position in its dealings with the Tamil people.

On November 28, the Sirisena government, which now has been in power for nearly three years, evoked the Prevention of Terrorism Act to arrest Tamils who had organized events to honor the memory of the fallen soldiers of the Tamil rebellion.

Maaveerar Naal has been observed annually since 1987 on November 27 to commemorate the day the first Tamil Tiger soldier was killed in action in 1982. The annual commemoration continued even after the rebellion was put down in May 2009. During the presidency of Mahinda Rajapaksa (2005-15), the event was observed in secret, as it was clear that the government would punish participants. But in November 2016, it was observed openly and was allowed to proceed.

The event in 2016 was attended by Tamil parliamentarians

and politicians. The Sri Lankan government's inclination to allow Tamils honour their sons and daughters killed in battle was widely regarded as a goodwill gesture toward the Tamil people and a signal to the world at large that the new regime was democratic in its approach.

However, last month, the Sri Lankan security forces actively engaged in intimidating people attending commemoration events across the northeast of the island – the Tamil homeland. Participants were photographed, people were warned that any display of Tamil Tiger symbols including photographs of the fallen in uniform was illegal, and there was a menacing army presence outside the premises where the commemoration events were conducted.

The very next day, Sri Lanka's state minister of defence, Ruwan Wijewardene, ordered the Terrorism Investigation Division, notorious for its use of torture, to investigate and arrest those involved in organizing the commemoration.

The heavy-handed response to this year's *Maaveerar Naal* by the Sirisena government comes in the wake of several other setbacks in the efforts to bring about an end to the conflict. These include the absence of any progress in respect of a 2015 UN Human Rights Council resolution to investigate war crimes committed during the latter stages of the civil war; delays in introducing a new constitution addressing the question of self-rule for the Tamil people; and the continuing spectre of torture of Tamils taken into custody.

UN Resolution

The UN resolution of 2015 was primarily focused on establishing a mechanism involving foreign judges in a local investigation probing war crimes committed during the latter stages of Sri Lanka's civil war. This was a further dilution of earlier resolutions calling for international investigation.

In March this year, Sri Lanka was given another two years to implement the proposals, but there is little evidence of any progress. On the contrary, Sirisena has stated categorically[1] that he will not make any "war hero" a suspect in cases of alleged war crimes. Addressing the Sri Lankan expatriate community in South Korea on November 28, he was dismissive of the UN resolution, stating[2]: "There won't be electric chairs, international tribunals or foreign judges. That book is closed."

New Constitution

The Sirisena government that replaced the Rajapaksa regime had agreed to address the root cause of the conflict via a new constitution to share political power with the Tamil people. The Tamil National Alliance, which had been in negotiations with the government, had understood the new constitution was to be "outside the unitary constitution amounting to federalism in substance."

However, Sirisena has since stated[3] categorically that he would never "betray the country" by introducing a federal constitution. This would mean that a new constitution, if implemented, would be unitary, ensuring that political power continues to reside with the majority Sinhala people. As it was this majoritarian rule that was the root cause of the conflict in the first place, a new unitary constitution is unlikely to resolve the conflict.

Torture

Early last month, an investigation by The Associated Press[4] found that more than 50 Tamil men had been raped, branded and tortured by the current government. The men were accused of trying to revive the Tamil Tigers rebel group and were tortured between early 2016 and July of this year, the report said.

There is some confusion as to whether the perpetrators were from the police or the army. Captors had identified[5] themselves as members of the Criminal Investigation Department, a police unit that investigates serious crimes. But some of the victims thought their captors and interrogators were soldiers.

Back to the Future

Almost three years after promising to address the issues that gave rise to the conflict and two years after co-sponsoring a resolution calling for a probe into the alleged war crimes, the Sri Lankan government has reverted to type, pandering to ultra-Sinhala nationalism. The situation in late 2017 appears to be no different to what prevailed before the conflict erupted into war in 1983.

Asia Times
16 February 2018

Hindutva takes on Tamil Nationalism.

The south Indian state of Tamil Nadu has become a battleground for the proponents of *Hindutva* and the champions of Tamil nationalism. *Hindutva* is the rallying cry of the Bharathiya Janata Party (BJP) and Rashtriya Swayamsevak Sangh (RSS),[1] a militant Hindu nationalist group that has for decades provided the shock troops for the BJP.

The BJP's approach is based on the assumption that the predominantly Hindu Tamils could be persuaded to embrace Hindu nationalism based on *Hindutva*, which calls for a homogeneous identity for all Hindus by eschewing other markers, languages and cultures.

Tamil Nationalism

This runs counter to Tamil nationalism, which derives its identity from language and rejects religion as a marker of Tamil identity.

The Dravida Munnetra Kazhagam (DMK), a political party founded in 1949, and several other Tamil nationalist parties and personalities have joined together in countering *Hindutva*. A DMK offshoot and political rival, the All India Anna Dravida Munnetra Kazhagam (AIADMK), the ruling party in Tamil Nadu, is in no position to take on the BJP, having imploded after the death of its charismatic leader Jayaram Jayalalithaa.

The success of the DMK and the AIADMK is a testimony to the potency of Tamil nationalism, which both parties have successfully exploited. In the hands of the DMK, Tamil nationalism became an ideology of mass mobilization.[2] This has enabled the DMK and the AIADMK to secure and hold political power for more than 50 years.

The Clash

In January, the latest clash between these two nationalisms was played out in two separate incidents. Central to both incidents was H Raja, the national secretary of the BJP, the ruling party federally.

In late January, at an event marking the release of a book by H Raja's father, a participant at the event, a Hindu priest, triggered a controversy[3] by not standing up when the Tamil anthem was played. Vijayendra Saraswathi remained seated even as other dignitaries such as the chief guest, Tamil Nadu Governor Banwarilal Purohit, stood up for the *Tamizh Thai Vazhthu*.

The Tamil anthem is sung or played at the beginning of

functions in Tamil Nadu. By not standing up, Vijayendra Saraswathi angered the public. Several public figures condemned the Hindu priest for disrespecting Tamil sentiments, and these notably included leading politicians across Tamil Nadu with strong nationalistic leanings.

Earlier in January, Vairamuthu, a Tamil scholar, speaking on Andal, one of the best-loved Hindu poet-saints of the Tamils, quoted from the 1978 book *Indian Movements: Some Aspects of Dissent, Protest and Reform*, which identified Andal as a *devadasi*. The term *devadasi* is open to interpretation; it could mean a female servant of a *deva* (god) or in a more pedestrian sense a temple prostitute.

The BJP's Raja mounted a vituperative attack by claiming that Vairamuthu had reduced the Hindu saint to a common prostitute. The attack gained momentum as several Andal devotees joined in, believing Vairamuthu had tarnished the image of Andal. This was met by a massive uproar against H Raja by Tamil nationalists who accused him of exploiting religious sentiments for political gain.

Political Vacuum

The BJP's evocation of *Hindutva* is an obvious attempt to capture power based on the perception that there is a political vacuum in Tamil Nadu. Since 1967, Tamil Nadu's politics has been dominated by two regional political parties, the DMK and AIADMK. Ever since the DMK captured political power in 1967, the state has been ruled by one of these two parties. In terms of policy and ideology, the two parties are similar. The distinction is largely attributable to the personalities of its leaders. Both parties have had charismatic leaders with mass appeal.

The DMK's M Karunanidhi has led the party since 1969, when he became leader after the death of its founder C N Annadurai. At the age of 92, Karunanidhi created history by winning his seat in the legislative assembly for the 13th time in a row in 2016. However, old age and ill health made him retire from politics.

The AIADMK owed its success to its own charismatic leaders, M G Ramachandran, who was its leader since his split from the DMK to form the new party in 1972 until his death in 1989. And thereafter Jayalalithaa led the party from 1989 until her untimely demise in December 2016 while in office.

Since then the AIADMK has been torn apart by a leadership struggle, while the DMK is yet to find a leader who can match Karunanidhi. M K Stalin, the son of Karunanidhi and heir apparent, is yet to prove himself.

Strategy and Tactics

It is this apparent political vacuum caused by the

departures of Jayalalithaa and Karunanidhi that seems to have rekindled the BJP's hopes of securing a foothold in Tamil Nadu. This sits well with the BJP's two-stage strategy[4] – electoral victory at the national level, which has been achieved, to be followed by similar success at the state level.

The tactics used by the proponents of *Hindutva* have been shaped by the RSS's tried and tested methods in northern India. In the north, it is not difficult to provoke anti-Islamic sentiment because of the widely held belief that conversions to Islam were made at the point of the sword, and memories of the horrendous clashes between Hindus and Muslims that took place during India's partition have not faded away. Anti-Christian sentiments are also much more pronounced in northern Indian states than in the southern states such as Tamil Nadu and Kerala, which have larger Christian populations and longer exposure to Christianity.

H Raja's tactics are predicated on the assumption that by labeling anyone expressing anti-BJP sentiments or by referring to his or her Islamic or Christian background, a religious divide could be perpetrated. Last October, Raja's attempt to discredit Tamil actor Vijay, who had been critical of the BJP's politics, by "outing" him as a Christian failed.

It is hard to refute the assessment by Ramu Manivannan,[5] head of the department of politics at the University of Madras, that the BJP has forfeited the opportunity to present itself as a potential alternative by embarking on polarizing tactics and intimidating strategies to gain access to political power.

The Diplomat
22 December 2017

Why Is Sri Lanka Defying the United Nations?

Sri Lanka's strategy of defiance, denial, and delay might be designed to evade the charge of genocide.

Lately, Colombo has intensified its defiance of UN resolutions calling for investigations into war crimes committed during the latter stages of the civil war. In late November, Sri Lankan President Maithripala Sirisena declared that[1] "There won't be electric chairs, international tribunals or foreign judges. That book is closed."

Earlier, in October, Colombo sought and obtained the help of British parliamentarian Lord Naseby to downplay a report by the UN Secretary General's Panel of Experts, which in March 2011 found "credible allegations" that as many as 40,000 civilians may have been killed in the final months of the civil war, mostly as a result of indiscriminate shelling by the Sri Lankan military. Naseby had called on the UN to reduce the number from 40,000 to between 7,000 and 8,000 based on his own research.

Naseby's links to Sri Lanka go back to 1975, when he founded the All-Party Parliamentary Group on Sri Lanka. Naseby has been an advocate for Sri Lanka in the British parliament and in 2005, was awarded *Sri Lanka Ratna,* the highest national honor bestowed upon foreigners for exceptional and outstanding service to the nation by the then Sri Lankan government. In November 2017, Sirisena thanked Naseby for calling for a reduction in numbers of the people killed. Although much has been made by the Sri Lankan press about Naseby's call for a revision of the casualties, this has been summarily dismissed by the British government via its High Commissioner in Colombo.

Britain's position is based on the Report of the UN Panel of Experts, comprising prominent human right activists, Marzuki Darusman (from Indonesia), Yasmin Sooka (South Africa), and Steven Ratner (United States). Unlike Naseby's "findings," the UN report has been corroborated by several other independent sources. These include: the Channel Four documentary *Killing Fields,* Francis Harrison's book *Still Counting the Dead,* and reports by Human Rights Watch and Amnesty International.

Since 2012, resolutions calling for international investigation into alleged war crimes in Sri Lanka have been passed in the UN. Until 2015, these were opposed by Colombo on the grounds that international investigations were intrusive and, if implemented, would undermine Sri Lanka's sovereignty. The Sri

Lankan government during this period was the one that had successfully crushed the Tamil rebellion and the resolutions passed were directed in particular at this government, headed by president Mahinda Rajapaksa.

In January 2015, Maithripala Sirisena, with the support of the United States and India, defeated Rajapaksa in the presidential election. The new regime was expected to be more receptive to UN resolutions on post-war justice. In September 2015, a new resolution calling for an investigation into war crimes avoided any reference to an international investigation and in its place called for establishing a mechanism involving foreign judges in a local investigation. The Sirisena government went along by co-sponsoring this resolution. However, in March 2017, Colombo sought and obtained another two years to implement the 2015 resolution. But its current actions show that it has no intention of implementing the resolution. Instead, it seeks defy the very resolution it had co-sponsored in 2015.

There are good reasons to suspect that the Sri Lankan government's opposition to any impartial investigation is due to its apprehension that it may result in Colombo having to face the much grimmer charge of genocide.

In February 2015, Sri Lanka's Tamil-dominated Northern Provincial Council passed a resolution reflecting Tamil sentiments that the crimes perpetrated went beyond war crimes and were in fact genocide. Following this resolution, the Office of the United Nations High

Commissioner for Human Rights (OHCHR) came under criticism for its "silence" on genocide. *The Hindu*, an Indian newspaper, was prompted to raise this with the OHCR, which responded by stating that the UN report does not preclude the potential for a future finding that genocide was committed as a result of further criminal investigations.[2]

OHCR's response was not entirely surprising. In December 2008, just six months before the Tamil rebellion was brutally crushed, the New York-based Genocide Prevention Project had identified Sri Lanka as one of the eight "red alert" countries where genocide and other mass atrocities were underway. And just two months later, in February 2009, the *Boston Globe* compared the ongoing massacre in Sri Lanka to the Bosnian Srebrenica genocide. Then there were the accusations levelled by Professor Francis A. Boyle[3], a leading American expert in international law, who interpreted the Sri Lankan government's actions as genocide under international law.[4]

In December 2013, a full session of the Rome-based Permanent Peoples Tribunal held in Bremen to consider evidence gained over three years found,"that the State of Sri Lanka is guilty of the crime of genocide against Eelam Tamils."[5]

Given the suspicions that Sri Lanka may well be guilty of genocide, this may be the reason for its concerted attempts to evade any kind of investigations into its conduct during the final phase of the war.

Asia Times
26 April 2018

Why Colombo Remains a Challenge for New Delhi

Former Sri Lankan president Mahinda Rajapaksa's resounding performance at the local-council elections in early February has prompted the observation that Rajapaksa is back in politics[1] and poised to regain political power. This is a blow to the "unity" government that replaced the Rajapaksa regime in January 2015.

The regime change that resulted in the formation of a "unity" government came about when former Rajapaksa loyalists joined the opposition right-leaning United National Party (UNP). The "unity" government suffered its first setback when a **Rajapaksa-backed**[2] no-confidence motion was made against Prime Minister Ranil Wickramasinghe on April 4, and 16 members of the "unity" government voted for the motion crossing the floor and taking their seats in the opposition benches.

Although the prime minister survived the motion, the government was weakened, with those 16 members who voted in favor of the no-confidence motion crossing[3] the floor and taking their seats in the opposition benches.

Regime Change

The regime change was welcomed by New Delhi and Washington. On January 9, 2015[4], even before the formal announcement of the election result, Indian Prime Minister Narendra Modi became the first foreign leader to call and congratulate the new president, Maithripala Sirisena, on his victory.

On the eve of the election, US secretary of state John Kerry had telephoned Rajapaksa to insist that he conduct a "free and fair election" and ensure a "peaceful" handover of power if Sirisena won the ballot. The high-level involvement by Washington in Sri Lanka's presidential election implied that US interests were at stake.

Both Washington and New Delhi had found the increasing influence of China over Sri Lanka under the Rajapaksa government to be a threat to their own influence in the strategically significant island nation.

Since late 2009, Washington had been deeply worried about Sri Lanka's drift toward China. A December 2009 US Senate Foreign Relations Committee report, "Sri Lanka: Re-charting US Strategy after the War," had noted that Sri Lanka's strategic drift toward China would have consequences for US interests in the region and that the United States could not afford to "lose" Sri Lanka. It called for increasing US leverage *vis-a-vis* Sri Lanka by adopting a multifaceted, broader and more robust approach to secure US interests. New Delhi became particularly concerned after Colombo, brushing aside India's concerns,[5] permitted two Chinese submarines to dock in Colombo within a space of seven weeks in late 2014.

As such, Washington and New Delhi had common grounds to welcome a change of government in Sri Lanka. Indeed, it has been suggested with some justification that New Delhi with Washington's backing had played an active role in the regime change.

Reports from Colombo[6] accused the chief of India's Research and Analysis Wing (RAW), K Ilango, of helping the opposition oust Rajapaksa as president. In the run-up to the presidential election, Ilango was transferred. In an interview given to an Indian journalist[7], Rajapaksa accused the West of working with RAW to oust him.

The regime change came about when Maithiripala Sirisena, a senior member of the Rajapaksa government, chose to defect with some members of his own party and challenge Rajapaksa at the presidential election of 2015. Although Sirisena won the election, he was unable to garner a majority of the Sinhala votes; he won because the Tamils and Muslims voted for him.

The Tamils had suffered immensely throughout Rajapaksa's rule, and later in his term, Muslims were subjected to state-condoned violence. Tamils voted for Sirisena for various reasons. Some believed that the Tamil National Alliance (TNA) had reached an understanding with Sirisena to implement a new constitution permitting self-rule for the Tamil-dominated northeast, while others were persuaded by Sirsena's promise to conduct an open inquiry into war-crimes allegations[8], and many who had lived under oppressive conditions for almost six years believed that a new administration would be an improvement..

Heavy voter turnout in the Tamil-majority areas of Sri Lanka has also been interpreted as a negative vote[9] cast against Rajapaksa. But there is no gainsaying that the challenge to oust Rajapaksa succeeded mainly because the Tamils voted for Sirisena.

Re-embrace of China

The regime change soon proved to be illusory for all those who had hoped to benefit. No attempt was made to address Tamil grievances. Colombo, having initially sought to balance its relationship with New Delhi and Beijing, soon began to tilt once again toward Beijing.

Sri Lanka's re-embrace of China is attributable to two factors. The first is China's debt-trap diplomacy[10], which involves providing large loans at commercial rates to countries like Sri Lanka to develop infrastructure projects in strategically significant locations. These loans are often extended in circumstances where the country is in no position to service them, forcing the borrower to lease back the asset to China.

In Sri Lanka, the management of Hambantota Port, which was built with Chinese loans, is no longer under the direct control of the Sri Lankan state. Its operation is controlled by China via its state-owned China Merchants Ports Holdings, to which Colombo sold a 70% stake as it was unable to meet its loan-repayment obligations.

Sri Lanka's re-embrace of China was also driven by another factor: the Sinhalese fear of India's interventionist agenda.

Ever since Sri Lanka became independent, its foreign policy has been driven by this fear of its giant neighbor. It is this perception about New Delhi that caused Sri Lanka to sign defense agreements permitting Britain the use of naval and air bases in Trincomalee immediately upon independence; take up a pro-Pakistani position during India's war against Pakistan in 1971; seek help from countries inimical to India during the early stages of the civil war; and surreptitiously involve China during the final phase of the war without letting India know.[11]

As far as Colombo is concerned, irrespective of the government in power, its foreign policy has always been underpinned by a compulsion to counter Indian influence.

India's response. Undeterred, New Delhi has tried to bring Colombo within its own sphere of influence either through coercion, as Indira Gandhi[12] did by arming Tamil rebels to exert pressure or through an alliance as the Indian government under Manmohan Singh attempted by helping Colombo defeat the Tamil rebels.

The latest attempt by the Indian government[13] to bring Colombo within its orbit through "regime change" failed because New Delhi failed to grasp that the majority-Sinhala nation harbors strong reservations and resentment[14] when it comes to India. These reservations were openly articulated by Dayan Jayatilleka, Sri Lanka's former envoy to the United Nations, when in April 2015 he declared that India is not Lanka's natural ally.[15]

Nevertheless, New Delhi is unlikely to give up on Colombo. But any such effort is bound to clash with Beijing's own robust agenda to establish its presence in Sri Lanka. Currently, Sri Lanka owes China US$8 billion of its total $65 billion of debt and as such[16] continues to be exposed to China's debt-trap diplomacy, not to mention Colombo's own desire to stay out of New Delhi's orbit.

For the foreseeable future, Colombo will continue to remain a challenge for New Delhi.

The Diplomat
3 May 2018

Can the Application of Universal Jurisdiction Foster Accountability in Sri Lanka?

A closer look at an important question.

At the 37th session of the Human Rights Council, which met in Geneva in February and March 2018, the High Commissioner for United Nations Human Rights Commission (UNHRC) Zeid Ra'ad Al-Hussein urged member states to explore other avenues to foster accountability in Sri Lanka including the application of universal jurisdiction[1]. The call was made in an attempt to bring about accountability for alleged war crimes committed during Sri Lanka's civil war in view of Sri Lanka's reluctance to comply with resolutions passed since March 2012.

UNHRC Resolutions

The March 2012 resolution was passed following findings by the UN Panel of Experts[2] in March 2011 that as many as 40,000 civilians may have been killed in the final months of the civil war, mostly as a result of indiscriminate shelling by the Sri Lankan military. In

March 2013, another resolution was passed encouraging Sri Lanka to conduct an independent and credible investigation into alleged war crimes.[3] In March 2014, the UN's Human Rights Council adopted a resolution[4] calling on Sri Lanka to undertake a comprehensive investigation into alleged serious violations and abuses of human rights and related crimes. The government of then-leader Mahinda Rajapaksa resisted the probe and denied U.N. officials entry to the island.[5] In the absence of any action, there was the expectation of a stronger resolution in March 2015. Instead, the UNHRC postponed the hearings to September 2015.

The UNHRC High Commissioner explained the reasons for the postponement, given the changing context in Sri Lanka[6] where a regime change had resulted in Rajapaksa being ousted and Maithripala Sirisena installed as president. The resolution passed at the September 2015 sessions called for a domestic accountability mechanism with international involvement.

In effect, a hybrid mechanism that was a far cry from the international investigation that the earlier resolutions had called for. Unlike previous resolutions, this time around Sri Lanka joined in passing the resolution as a co-sponsor prompting John Kerry, then-U.S. Secretary of State to declare "This resolution marks an important step toward a credible transitional justice process, owned by Sri Lankans and with the support and involvement of the international community."[7]

In March 2017 at the 34th session of the Human Rights Council, Colombo was granted a further extension of two years to probe alleged war crimes committed during the civil war. Instead, the Sri Lankan regime not only failed to implement the resolution it had co-sponsored in September 2015, but in January 2016, President Sirisena during an interview with *Al Jazeera*'s Hoda Abdel-Hamid[8] flatly denied the war crimes allegation, referring only to "human rights violations." Later, in November 2017, Sirisena went a step further declaring "There won't be electric chairs, international tribunals or foreign judges. That book is closed."[9]

The High Commissioner's Call for 'Other Avenues'

Faced with this defiance, UNHRC's High Commissioner in despair[10] called upon member states to explore other avenues to foster accountability in Sri Lanka.

Sri Lanka is a signatory to the Geneva Convention, which prohibits war crimes. However, Sri Lanka is not a signatory to the Rome Statute that created the International Criminal Court (ICC) in 2002 to prosecute individuals for serious crimes, such as war crimes. As such, for Sri Lanka's alleged war criminals to be brought before the ICC, the UN Security Council has to refer Sri Lanka to the ICC. This matter is fraught with geopolitical interests of various parties, primarily China and the United who are permanent members of the Security Council and are committed to strengthen their own relationships with Colombo.

This leaves UNHRC with the other option: universal jurisdiction. The term refers to the idea[11] that a national court may prosecute individuals for any serious crime against international law — such as crimes against humanity, war crimes, genocide, and torture — based on the principle that such crimes harm the international community or international order itself.

But, actions do not succeed where the alleged criminal enjoys diplomatic immunity.

On October 24, 2011, an Australian citizen, Arunachalam Jegatheeswaran, filed an indictment[12] against Sri Lanka's President Mahinda Rajapaksa, Jegatheeswaran alleged that Rajapaksa had deliberately targeted civilians and civilian infrastructure (hospitals, schools and community centers) in 2007 and 2008 and that this amounted to war crimes and crimes against humanity. The charges were laid in the Melbourne Magistrates' Court on the eve of Rajapaksa's arrival in Australia for the Commonwealth Heads of Government Meeting (CHOGM). Within a day of filing the indictment, the case was quashed by the Attorney-General on the grounds that "continuation of the proceedings would be in breach of domestic law and Australia's obligations under international law" specifically that the prosecution of Rajapaksa would breach Australian and international laws that provide immunity from criminal prosecution for heads of state.

Jagath Dias, a former Sri Lankan Army Commander was withdrawn from the Sri Lankan Embassy in Berlin[13] in September 2011 where he had held the position of a deputy ambassador for Germany, Switzerland and the Vatican. The withdrawal followed the submission of a comprehensive dossier substantiating war crimes committed by Dias to the German Federal Foreign Office by the European Center for Constitutional and Human Rights (ECCHR) in January 2011.

Then there was the case of former General Jagath Jayasuriya who was Sri Lanka's ambassador to Brazil, Colombia, Peru, Chile, Argentina and Suriname . On August 28, 2017[14], human rights groups in South America filed war crimes lawsuits against the general. The action was spearheaded by the International Truth and Justice Project (ITJP), an evidence-gathering organisation based in South Africa. On 29 August 2017, Jagath Jayasuriya fled back to Sri Lanka. According Ms Sooka of ITJP, "He was tipped off, and he skipped from Brazil."[15]

Universal jurisdiction, unlike the ICC, is a blunt instrument when it comes to bringing alleged war criminals to trial. It can at times help, but is hampered by diplomatic immunity where the alleged war criminal is a diplomat or a head of state. Even when the alleged perpetrator is not protected by diplomatic immunity, states are reluctant to permit the application of universal jurisdiction as it can harm state-to-state relations. As Frances Harrison of the ITJP pointed out in an interview with the Sri Lanka-based think tank, Centre for Strategic Studies Trincomalee[16], "it would be good if the diplomats, donors, judicial authorities and UN had a more coordinated approach – one that continues to pressure the government of Sri Lanka to act on its transitional justice commitments while developing a parallel track of really supporting universal jurisdiction actions."

Asia Times
16 July 2018

Sri Lanka's Chinese Connection: Beyond Bribes and Debts

Former Sri Lankan president Mahinda Rajapaksa's ambition was to build a port in his own district of Hambantota. Although feasibility studies showed the port to be commercially unviable, Beijing extended credit to build it.

When Rajapaksa's presidency was challenged in late 2014, Beijing, concerned that a new regime might be an obstacle to its plans, dispensed payments directly to campaign aides and activities for Rajapaksa, who had agreed to China's terms.[1] Although Rajapaksa was voted out, in the face of mounting debt, the new regime was compelled to lease the port to a Chinese government-owned company for 99 years. This explains how Sri Lanka's Hambantota port came under Chinese control.

Unanswered Questions

But it does not tell how Beijing was able to foster a close relationship with Colombo under the nose of New Delhi, the dominant regional power. Nor does it explain why the new regime in Colombo, which had begun by wanting to pursue a balanced approach, continued the tilt toward

Beijing. This became evident in late 2015 when Colombo agreed to buy military transport airplanes from China [2] and even clearer in early April 2016 when Sri Lankan Prime Minister Ranil Wickramasinghe, renewing the Chinese-funded Colombo Port City project, declared that the cooperation between China and Sri Lanka would intensify and go far beyond that.[3]

During 2017, New Delhi attempted to gain a foothold in southern Sri Lanka by offering to purchase 70% of Mattala International Airport, dubbed "the world's emptiest international airport," on a 40-year lease. There was no commercial benefit for India. It was an offer similar to the one that saw Hambantota port come under Chinese management.

Colombo did not respond. Had Colombo been serious about balancing Beijing against New Delhi, this could have been a worthwhile opportunity. Nor did Colombo respond to New Delhi's overtures about operating a major oil-storage facility and a liquefied natural gas (LNG) plant in Trincomalee in addition to developing the Port of Trincomalee as a key transit point.

In January 2015, there was speculation about Rajapaksa's demise resulting in a regime likely to be friendlier toward New Delhi, but not everyone agreed. Nitin Pai of the Takshashila Institution, an independent think-tank, argued that in view of the geopolitical underpinnings of the Beijing-Colombo axis, it was unlikely that Sri Lanka's relationship with China would change merely because one president was replaced by another. Colombo is unlikely to give up on the strategic gains made through forging a close relationship with China rooted in its policy born out of historic antipathy to India, its giant neighbor.

Politics of Fear

This antipathy can be traced to Sri Lanka's first prime minister, D S Senanayake, who feared that the most likely threat to Sri Lanka's independence would come from India. Senanayake associated this fear of India with the presence of Tamils in a region in Sri Lanka not far from southern India, home to more than 50 million Tamils at that time.

During pre-independence discussions with Lord Soulbury, the head of the commission appointed by the British to draft a constitution for the island, Senanayake expressed his fear about the Tamils in Sri Lanka confederating with India "as Ulster separated from the Irish Republic to federate with Britain."

According to Sri Lankan historian K M de Silva, the defense agreements signed in 1947 with Whitehall in the wake of the transfer of power from Britain were part of Colombo's "process of adjusting to the uncertainties of a new pattern of international politics in South Asia with India as an independent state." And John Gooneratne, a former Sri Lankan diplomat, wrote in *A Decade of Confrontation*: "There was always a tension between Sri Lanka and India as it usually exists where a small state is juxtaposed next to a very big state. And, in the post-independence period, there was a constant awareness of the presence of a very big northern neighbor projecting its power in the south."

Colombo has always countered its giant neighbor's influence by forging close relationships with those opposed to New Delhi. During the Indo-Pakistani War of 1971, Sri Lanka supported Pakistan by providing refueling facilities. During the Cold War, Colombo maintained either a strictly non-aligned position or a pro-Western policy in contrast to New Delhi, which had a special relationship with the Soviet Union.

By the early 1980s, Colombo's suspicions seemed justified when New Delhi armed and trained Tamil rebels to exert pressure on Sri Lanka, which was showing clear signs of moving into the Western camp.

These suspicions were only reinforced when India intervened directly in 1987 under the Indo-Sri Lanka Accord to deny the US the use of Trincomalee Harbor and permission to set up a Voice of America broadcasting facility in Sri Lanka. In return, the Indian army attempted to disarm the Tamil rebels spearheaded by the Liberation Tigers of Tamil Eelam (LTTE), better known as the Tamil Tigers. But this ended in disaster for the Indian forces, which, unable to disarm the LTTE, left the island after suffering almost a thousand casualties.

Politics of Duplicity

After its costly intervention in the late 1980s, New Delhi ceased to play a direct role in Sri Lanka's armed conflict. That was until 2008, when New Delhi renewed its direct intervention, this time to defeat the Tamil Tigers.

Piecing together two separate narratives, one by Sam Rajappa, a long-term journalist with The Statesman, and the other by Lalith Weeratunga, secretary to the Sri Lankan president, Mahinda Rajapaksa, it is possible to understand how Colombo was able to counter New Delhi's influence by securing Chinese assistance. Both accounts are highly credible, providing in great detail the events leading to New Delhi's direct intervention.

According to <u>Sam Rajappa</u>[4], the chain of events leading to New Delhi providing military assistance to Colombo began with a preliminary meeting between Rajapaksa's emissaries and a group of four Tamil Nadu civil-society representatives. This was followed by several other meetings during which both parties reached a unanimous understanding that a military victory for one side without a political strategy to address the grievances of the Tamil people was unlikely to produce a lasting solution.

Rajappa refers to two meetings that Tamil Nadu civil-society members had with Rajapaksa on July 17, 2007, and on March 25, 2008, in Colombo and Rajapaksa fully endorsing the view that the solution to the conflict should emerge from within Sri Lanka refined through Indian opinion.

The dynamics changed when New Delhi became aware of this initiative and New Delhi intervened by signaling to the Sri Lankan government that it should go all out to decimate the LTTE without insisting on a political solution. Rajappa attributes this decision by New Delhi to Sonia Gandhi, who wanted LTTE leader Velupillai Pirapaharan and its intelligence chief, Pottu Amman, dead and had pledged all military support for Sri Lanka to achieve this goal. The national security adviser, M K Narayanan, and the foreign secretary, Shivshankar Menon, are identified by Rajappa as responsible for implementing this course of action that served "Sonia Gandhi's interest above national interest."[5]

Lalith Weeratunge's account in June corroborates Sam Rajappa's account of July 2011. According to Weeratunge,[6] the initial contact on behalf of the Indian government was made sometime in 2008 by India's high commissioner, Alok Prasad.

At this meeting, Sri Lanka's president was asked to nominate three individuals who would then meet three of their Indian counterparts. Rajapaksa's nominees were Basil Rajapaksa, senior adviser to the president, Gotabaya Rajapaksa, the defense secretary, and himself, the secretary to the president. New Delhi had nominated M K Narayanan, the national security adviser, Shankar Menon, the foreign secretary, and Vijay Singh, the defense secretary. This was India's troika to engage with Sri Lanka's troika to monitor the war against the Tamil Tigers. The teams from both countries were made up of individuals who had the ear of their leaders.

Having met for the first time at the Taj Samudra hotel in Colombo, they met several times thereafter. Weeratunge makes special mention of the camaraderie during these meetings and how they continued for a while after the defeat of the Tamil Tigers. Having pointedly referred to Narayanan's admiration for Gothabaya Rajapaksa, Weeratunge notes that as the war progressed, Colombo found itself in a commanding position vis-à-vis New Delhi. Emboldened by this shift in power, Rajapaksa promptly dismissed Narayanan's request in April 2009 to stop military activity in the north of Sri Lanka to accommodate state government elections in Tamil Nadu to be held in mid-May that year.

Having reached a situation in which New Delhi was well entrenched as a willing partner, Colombo sought and obtained Beijing's assistance. According to Brahma Chellaney[7] in an essay titled "Behind the Sri Lankan Bloodbath," this assistance from China was obtained by Sri Lanka "through adroit but duplicitous diplomacy.[8]" Colombo assured India it would approach other arms suppliers only if New Delhi couldn't provide a particular weapon system it needed. Yet it quietly began buying arms from China without letting India know.

It is hard to refute that New Delhi's flawed foreign policy was a crucial factor in the bloodbath that ensued. At the same time, this self-serving foreign policy driven by Sonia Gandhi has significantly diminished New Delhi's influence over Sri Lanka.

The Diplomat
19 September 2018

Unsilenced: Male Rape by the Sri Lankan Security Forces

A new report documents the widespread use of sexual torture on male Tamil detainees.

The latest report titled *Unsilenced*[1], released by the International Truth and Justice Project (ITJP) on September 19, makes for grim reading. The report addresses a form of torture that is rarely spoken about despite being widely practiced – sexual violence against men caught up in conflicts. The report is by Dr. Heleen Touquet, a researcher and an assistant professor at the faculty of Social Sciences at the University of Leuven, Belgium.

The study by ITJP focuses on the so-called "post conflict" era in Sri Lanka from 2009 to date, a period of almost 10 years since the war ended. The report makes it painfully clear that this particular mode of torture is widely practiced by the Sri Lankan security forces. Most importantly, it challenges the commonly held notion that it is women who are primarily subject to sexual violence as part of conflict-related sexual abuse.

Dr. Chris Dolan, who has worked with male survivors

of conflict-related sexual violence, notes in his foreword to the report that the weight of evidence of systematic abuse contained in the pages of this report undermines any assumption that those in overall command had no responsibility for this type of torture.

There have been other reports in the past that have identified male rape as a form of torture used by the Sri Lankan authorities. The issue was raised in the Freedom from Torture Reports in 2012 and 2015, the 2013 Human Rights Watch Report, and the 2016 report on Sri Lanka by the UN Special Rapporteur on Torture. In fact, the UN report concluded[2] that men in detention in Sri Lanka were as likely to be subjected to sexual violence as female detainees.

But the ITJP report is different in that it focuses just on male victims and provides detailed narratives of the type of torture. The report also exposes the strategic use of sexual torture engaged by the perpetrators — Sri Lanka's security forces.

Unsilenced is based on 121 testimonials, all by Tamil men from Sri Lanka. The ITJP's work for this project has been time consuming and challenging. It required trained investigators to spend considerable amount of time with the victims to build trust. On an average] each investigator needed to spend four to five hours per day over three or four days to build this trust. Survivors were willing to speak about their experiences because ITJP could guarantee strict privacy and often the disclosure itself proved to be cathartic. At the same time, as a general rule the victims would not disclose this type of torture to members of their family given the stigma attached to it in Tamil culture.

The alleged perpetrators were from different branches across the Sri Lankan security establishment, including the Terrorist Investigation Division (TID), Criminal Investigation Department (CID), and different branches of the military. While most perpetrators were men, according to the victims, there were also many women involved in sexual abuse of male prisoners.

As one of the survivors told ITJP:

> *I was also interrogated by a female intelligence officer who badly tortured me. She was in uniform. She beat me with batons. She was the worst torturer. She sexually tortured me. She stamped on my private parts and she beat me with sticks on my private parts. She tied my penis with thin thread and pulled it.*

The sexual abuse of Tamil men has taken place in many locations: rehabilitation centers, army camps, prisons, detention centers, and houses. Joseph Camp, where detainees were held soon after the war, and Boosa, the prison for men arrested under the notorious Prevention of Terrorism Act, were often cited as places where this type of torture took place.

Unsilenced draws attention to the Office of the High Commissioner for Human Rights Investigation on Sri Lanka (OISL), which concluded that incidents of sexual violence were not isolated acts, but part of a deliberate policy to inflict torture to obtain information, intimidate, and inflict fear.

The report is replete with detailed accounts of sexual torture. Below is an example:

> *Two new men came into my room. I saw their faces when they opened the door. They removed my clothes. I was standing against the wall. They removed all my clothes, my shirt, trousers, and underwear. One was wearing a t-shirt and the other a white collared shirt, and both had brown police type trousers. They didn't say anything. I was able to see that they lowered their trousers. They began to rape me.*

According to *Unsilenced,* this type sexual torture falls into distinct categories that included forced nudity, genital mutilation, rape, and coerced sexual acts. While all of them were humiliating, genital mutilation appeared to be the most painful. Coerced sexual acts were both painful and humiliating, as it involved male detainees forced to have sex with each other or rape a female inmate. In many cases the abuse was public, with several officers watching while the victims abused each other.

The mental, physical, and social consequences of such sexual abuse are enormous. Of all the torture they had gone through, it was the sexual violence that affected the male survivors most. It manifested itself in memories that disrupted their daily lives. Because sexual abuse is associated with shame and the social stigma attached to it, many victims believed they were contaminated and unfit for marriage. The already-married men were inclined to keep the extent of the abuse from their wives. As one of them put it,

I had a lot of pain in my anus. I was bleeding. I did not tell my wife that I was raped, only that I was detained and beaten. These are not things you can say to your wife. You do not talk about these things in my culture and she would be worried and upset. She was pregnant and I did not want to upset her.

The report concludes that sexual abuse of Tamil men in detention in Sri Lanka is massive and widespread and has occurred throughout the conflict and the post conflict period.

Unsilenced ends by noting that, given the political environment in Sri Lanka with its stalled reconciliation process, ongoing massive abuses of human rights, and impunity for war crimes, the situation is not conducive for this issue to be addressed locally.

Asia Times
12 October 2018

Sri Lanka's Tamil Cause, a Political Football?

On 20 September this year, Tamil Nadu's ruling All India Dravida Munnetra Kazhagam (AIADMK) declared that the opposition Dravida Munnetra Kazhagam (DMK) and the Congress party were responsible for the genocide in Sri Lanka and demanded that the DMK and Congress be tried as "international war criminals[1] AIADMK's charge was dismissed by the DMK as blatantly political as it was made immediately following the allegation of 'corruption' within the ruling party.

AIADMK's apparent rationale for raising the issue of war crimes and genocide at this point in time was based on so called 'revelations' by former Sri Lankan President Mahinda Rajapaksa. Earlier in September, during his visit to India, Rajapaksa[2] had wanted the Indian Prime Minister Narendra Modi to renew the "abiding friendship" forged between Sri Lanka and India during the final war against the Liberation Tigers of Tamil Eelam (LTTE). This seemed enough for the AIADMK to remind the people of DMK's complicity in the atrocities committed during the war as it was then a major ally of the ruling Congress party at the centre.

Indeed, there is much to suggest the Sri Lankan regime was guilty of war crimes and even genocide. The report by the UN Panel of Experts Report had estimated in 2011 that the number of civilians killed to be around 40,000. In her book *Still Counting the Dead,* Frances Harrison, a former BBC journalist, had identified war crimes that included luring civilians into so called 'Safety Zones' and then deliberately bombing these areas. Sri Lanka's war crimes were also exposed by *"No Fire Zone"* a 96-minute Emmy-nominated feature documentary released in November 2013. In its report dated 29 September 2018, the International Truth and Justice Project (ITJP) had identified the use of cluster bombs by the Sri Lankan air force, also a war crime.

Pointedly ignoring that the invitation to Rajapaksa had been extended by Subramanian Swamy[3], a senior MP of the Bharathiya Janatha Party (BJP) ruling at the centre, Tamil Nadu's head of the BJP, Tamilisai Soundarrajan, weighed in, saying that the DMK and the Congress had committed war crimes. This in turn has evoked a sharp reaction from the DMK, prompting its spokesperson KS Radhakrishnan[4] to question why Prime Minister Modi had welcomed Rajapaksa, widely regarded in Tamil Nadu as the perpetrator of war crimes committed against Sri Lanka's Tamils.

The inclination of Tamil Nadu's politicians and political parties to evoke the plight of Sri Lanka's Tamisl to gain political mileage is nothing new. Both the AIADMK and the DMK, the major political parties have routinely exploited this issue to gain political support.

Before its implosion following the untimely death of its charismatic leader, Ms Jayalalithaa Jeyaram, the AIADMK had established itself as the champion of Sri Lanka's Tamils. AIADMK was able to obliterate the DMK at the May 2011 State Elections because it was able to accuse the DMK as being complicit in the massacres in the final stages of the war in 2009. In June 2011, the Tamil Nadu Assembly, now dominated by the AIADMK, adopted a unanimous resolution seeking imposition of economic sanctions against Sri Lanka. Again in 2013, Tamil Nadu's assembly passed a resolution calling for the establishment of a separate state for the Tamils of Sri Lanka. In the 2014 General Elections, AIADMK swept the polls winning 37 of the seats with another regional party also with strong Tamil nationalistic leanings securing another seat. BJP was able to secure just one seat in Tamil Nadu at an election where it had performed exceptionally well India-wide to form a government on its own right.

It was clear Tamil Nadu was marching to a different beat driven by the massacres of fellow Tamils in Sri Lanka. AIADMK was determined to continue cashing on it. Consequently, in September 2015, a resolution was sponsored by the AIADMK at the state assembly characterizing charges against Sri Lanka as 'war crimes and genocide'[5]. The 2016 state elections justified AIADMK's stance, helping it beat its rival and defy the trend in Tamil Nadu since 1984 of voting out the incumbent party.

But in recent times the AIADMK has largely ignored the situation of Sri Lanka's Tamils. Instead, it has been consumed by its internal issues and dealing with its political unpopularity. Rajapaksa's visit and his remarks implicating the former Congress led Indian government in the final stages of the war against the Tamils had provided the AIADMK with some ammunition to fight the DMK.

AIADMK of 2018, unlike when it was under the leadership of Jayalalithaa is a weak party riven by internal squabbles. As such is forced to rely on the patronage of the BJP government at the centre. It is widely speculated that it may form a coalition with the BJP to contest the 2019 General Election. Should this prove true, AIADMK will be constrained in appealing to Tamil nationalistic sentiments given the contest between *Hindutva* and Tamil nationalism in Tamil Nadu[6].

This would leave the DMK free to exploit these sentiments by focusing on its past when it was a strong champion of the 'Tamil Eelam' cause. This includes its chief M Karunanidhi's refusal to receive the Indian Peace Keeping Forces (IPKF) upon its return having failed to disarm the Tamil Tigers. Karunanidhi's boycott of the IPKF was on the grounds that the IPKF had during its 'peacekeeping' mission in Sri Lanka "killed thousands of innocent Tamils and raped Tamil women"[7]. Notwithstanding his past record, the same Karunanidhi's failure to prevent the massacre of Tamils in Sri Lanka.is likely to haunt the party. But with the demise of Karunanidhi and many Tamil nationalist in its ranks, the DMK may well be able to counter this particular disadvantage.

The stance of the major parties has been largely opportunistic. But, since May 2009 there has been a qualitative difference in the sentiments in Tamil Nadu. Whereas, prior to the 'genocide' , the support for Sri Lanka's Tamils was more in sympathy, the sentiments now are fuelled by the conviction that these fellow Tamils need to be rescued and the perpetrators punished. The Dravidian political parties can no longer treat the issue simply as a factor in their political calculations. They are obliged to act on their promises should they wish to continue their domination of Tamil Nadu politics as they have in the last six decades.

The Diplomat
30 October 2018

Sri Lanka's Constitutional Crisis: The Geopolitical Dimension

The sacking of Sri Lanka's prime minister bodes poorly for India and the US, but is a welcome sign for China.

The entire country, not to mention the international community, was taken unawares on October 25 when Sri Lanka's President Maithripala Sirisena sacked Prime Minister Ranil Wickramasinghe and replaced him with Mahinda Rajapaksa, the former president.

It was widely known that there has been tension between Sirisena and Wickramasinghe for quite some time. Relations worsened following the local elections in February this year, when the ruling coalition performed badly and Sirisena blamed Wickramasinghe. In March, Sirisena relived Wickramasinghe of several institutions under prime ministerial control, including the country's Central Bank.

Adding an international dimension, the major point of contention between the president and the prime minister revolved around the delays in implementing joint projects agreed upon between Sri Lanka and India. Whereas Wickramasinghe remained committed to implementing the projects, Sirisena was not. At a cabinet meeting[1] on October 17, Sirisena and Wickramasinghe clashed over handing over to India the development of the East Terminal of the Colombo port.

Sirisena Takes Control

In November 2014, Sirisena, then the minister of health in the Rajapaksa-led United Peoples Freedom Alliance (UPFA), had surprised Rajapaksa by aligning himself with the Wickramasinghe-led United National Party (UNP) to challenge Rajapaksa at the presidential elections in January 2015. Sirisena won that contest mainly because he had the support of the UNP and Sri Lanka's Tamil and Muslim communities. Rajapaksa was defeated, despite receiving a majority of Sinhalese votes.

That particular change in government was welcomed by New Delhi and Washington. On January 9, 2015[2], even before the formal announcement of the election results, Indian Prime Minister Narendra Modi became the first foreign leader to call and congratulate Sirisena on his victory. India had been worried about the Rajapaksa administration's tilt toward Beijing. New Delhi became particularly concerned after Colombo, brushing aside India's concerns[3], permitted two Chinese submarines to dock in Colombo within a space of seven weeks in late 2014.

On the eve of the election, then-U.S. Secretary of

State John Kerry had telephoned[4] Rajapaksa to insist that he conduct a "free and fair election" and ensure a "peaceful" handover of power should Sirisena win the ballot. The high-level involvement by Washington in Sri Lanka's presidential election was not surprising. The United States had been deeply worried about Sri Lanka's drift toward China under the Rajapaksa presidency for years. A December 2009 U.S. Senate Foreign Relations Committee report, "Sri Lanka: Re-charting US Strategy after the War," noted that Sri Lanka's strategic drift toward China would have consequences for U.S. interests in the region and stated that "the United States cannot afford to 'lose' Sri Lanka." It called for increasing U.S. leverage vis-a-vis Sri Lanka by adopting a multifaceted, broader, and more robust approach to secure U.S. interests.

In an interview given to an Indian journalist,[5] Rajapaksa accused the West of working with the Research and Analysis Wing (RAW), India's intelligence service to oust him.

The new administration was successful in introducing the 19th amendment to the Sri Lankan constitution, which limited the president to two terms and stripped the president of the power to dismiss the prime minister. The former ensured Rajapaksa, having already served two terms, could not return to power and the latter appeared to secure Wickramasinghe continuing as prime minister.

Much to the disappointment of India in particular, Sirisena showed little enthusiasm to stem Colombo's drift toward Beijing. In late 2016 Sri Lanka agreed to buy military transport airplanes from China;[6] the next year Colombo signed a deal give 70 percent of the Hambantota deep seaport[7] on a 99-year lease to China for $1.1 billion. The Sirisena government also offered to renew the Chinese-funded Colombo Port Project, which had been suspended after the transfer of power. Meanwhile, Sirisena's government continued to delay implementing several India-funded projects, a policy in keeping with that of former President Rajapaksa. At the same time Sirisena ruled out any alliance with Rajapaksa loyalists on the grounds that they will not join him to form a government.[8]

Still, it soon became clear that Sirisena's anti-Delhi position had hardened. Matters came to a head on October 16, 2018 when Sirisena accused India's RAW of plotting his assassination,[9] an allegation described as "wild and bizarre"[10] by the chairman of *The Hindu*, a leading Indian national newspaper. Sirisena later told Modi in a phone call that "his words had been misquoted and distorted," and "denied having said that Indian agencies would be involved in the case in any manner," according to an Indian government spokesperson.[11]

Rajapaksa Rises Again

Sirisena's subsequent action of dismissing his prime minister and appointing his nemesis Rajapaksa to that position proved to be even stranger than the RAW accusations. That decision has the potential to completely reverse the election results of 2015 – which were seen as stemming Colombo's drift toward Beijing and helping New Delhi reassert its role as the regional hegemon.

Beijing promptly demonstrated its satisfaction with the developments. Chinese President Xi Jinping[12] emerged as one of the first world leaders to congratulate the newly appointed Prime Minister Mahinda Rajapaksa.

The first reaction from India came not from the prime minister but from Subramaniam Swamy, an upper house member of the Bharathiya Janatha Party (BJP), India's ruling party. Swamy congratulated Rajapaksa and suggested that India "would benefit by having good ties with Sri Lanka under Rajapaksa's leadership.[13]

But this does not appear to be the position of the Indian government. New Delhi is constrained in dealing with a government in which Rajapaksa is prime minister, and not only because of his well-known anti-Indian outlook[14]. It is also constrained by the strong anti-Rajapaksa sentiments prevailing in the south Indian state of Tamil Nadu, where all political parties and key political figures[15] have unanimously condemned Rajapaksa's appointment, citing his role in war crimes and mass atrocities committed against Tamils in 2009. Having maintained silence for two days, New Delhi[16] responded cautiously by calling for the constitutional process to be respected and extending its developmental assistance to Sri Lanka.

Washington was more forthright in its response, urging Sirisena to "immediately reconvene parliament"[17] to allow legislators to quell the constitutional crisis sparked by the sacking of Prime Minister Ranil Wickramasinghe. The European Union joined the United States and the United Kingdom to urge political parties in Sri Lanka to abide by the constitution, which (as mentioned earlier) forbids the president from ousting the prime minister.

Given Sri Lanka's strategic location in the India Ocean, the interest shown in recent developments by New Delhi, Beijing, and Washington comes as no surprise.

Asia Times
5 December 2018

An evaluation of Sri Lanka's Democratic Credentials

On Monday, Sri Lanka's Court of Appeal issued an interim injunction suspending the government of Mahinda Rajapaksa, his ministers, deputy ministers, and state ministers from continuing to function in their respective portfolios. This has reversed, albeit temporarily, President Maithripala Sirisena's attempt on October 26 to re-install a government under former president Rajapaksa as prime minister.

Earlier, Sirisena's attempt to dissolve Parliament in the absence of a majority supporting Rajapaksa was stayed by the Supreme Court until December 7. These actions no doubt demonstrate the independence of the country's judiciary, an essential attribute of a democracy.

Sri Lanka's constitutional crisis was triggered by Sirisena appointing former president Mahinda Rajapaksa as the country's new prime minister on October 26, in effect firing the sitting prime minister, Ranil Wickramasinghe. The removal of a sitting prime minister is a clear violation of the country's constitution, that is if one is to rely on the English version of it. This is because the Sinhala version of the constitution appears to provide the president with the power to remove the prime minister.

In such circumstances, where there is a discrepancy between the Sinhala version and the Tamil or English versions of the constitution, the law clearly stipulates that it is the Sinhala version that will prevail. It is argued that the import of the Sinhala version is the same[1] as the English version and the discrepancy is attributable to the chaotic legislative process[2] by which the 19th Amendment to the constitution defining the president's powers was enacted in 2015.

However, this is yet to be tested in court. In view of the independence demonstrated by the judiciary to date, it may well result in actions that resolve Sri Lanka's constitutional crisis.

Should that occur, much will be made about Sri Lanka's democracy and its restoration. This is because from the very beginning Sri Lanka's constitutional crisis was framed as a challenge to democracy.

Indeed, Sri Lanka is widely described as one of Asia's oldest democracies[3]. No doubt this perception is backed by Sri Lanka's current constitution, which was enacted in 1978, and its previous constitutions, the founding 1948 charter and the 1972 republican constitution, being underpinned by features associated with democracy, that is, parliamentary assemblies, periodic elections and an independent judiciary.

But do they make Sri Lanka a democracy? The country's laws providing supremacy to the Sinhala version of the constitution should surely cause some niggling doubts about Sri Lanka's democratic credentials.

Ethnocracy not Democracy

Upon a close examination of Sri Lanka's constitutions enacted in 1948, 1972 and 1978, it becomes obvious that Sri Lanka cannot be regarded as a democracy but has to be considered an ethnocracy. Ethnocracy basically means[4] "government or rule by an ethnic group" or *ethnos*, and more precisely rule by a particular *ethnos* in a multi-ethnic situation where there is at least one other significant ethnic group.

Indeed, since it was granted its independence by Britain in 1948, Sri Lanka has emerged as a typical ethnocracy[5] in which the state apparatus is appropriated by the dominant ethnic group to further its own interests, power and resources. In Sri Lanka's case, Sinhala Buddhist ethnicity is the key to securing political power. As such, resolving the constitutional crisis is not a matter of restoring democracy but of restoring ethnocracy.

Indeed, over the years Sri Lanka's ethnocracy has been strengthened by constitutions enacted by succeeding Sinhala-dominated governments. It is not surprising therefore that Oren Yiftachel of Ben-Gurion University and Asad Ghanem of the University of Haifa, in an article[6] titled "Understanding 'ethnocratic regimes: the politics of seizing contested territories," identified Sri Lanka as an ethnocratic state.

An ethnocratic state, however, is not completely devoid of democracy. But this democracy is confined to the dominant ethnic group. As pointed out by James Anderson[7] of Queens University Belfast, within an ethnocratic state the dominant *ethnos* "typically *demands* democracy, actively wants it – at least for itself."

"Thus these national regimes are not simply authoritarian: they typically have parliamentary assemblies and periodic elections, for instance, and perhaps a (sometimes ostensibly?) independent judiciary, and a (supposedly?) free media. These can give the appearance of 'ordinary democracy' but they hide a 'deeper structure' which is profoundly *anti*-democratic in that the democracy applies only or mainly to politics *within the dominant ethnos*, not to the *demos* of all the people in the state territory.

"Rule is mainly or solely by members and representatives of that *ethnos*, it is they who are in charge, making the major decisions: *ethnos* and demos are conflated but the 'democracy' is disproportionately and sometimes exclusively available to the favored *ethnos*. And it is this political cleavage between the ethnic groups which defines the character of the state as ethnocratic rather than democratic."

Sri Lanka exhibits all of the above.

Sri Lanka's Constitution(s)

The evaluation of Sri Lanka's current constitution and the previous two constitutions by Andrea Iff, a Swiss academic and political scientist, confirms that all of Sri Lanka's constitutions have been based on ethnocratic principles.

In a chapter titled "Constitutional Accommodation vs Integration in Sri Lanka" in *Sri Lanka: 60 Years of Independence and Beyond,* Iff makes it clear that the so-called democracy that is being associated with Sri Lanka is illusionary. Having painstakingly examined Sri Lanka's 1948, 1972 and the 1978 constitutions, she concludes that all of Sri Lanka's constitutions have been based on a "control model" where the majority segment dominates and reduces all other segments to a position of subordination.

Sri Lanka's flag is a powerful symbolic reiteration of this truth. The flag is dominated by a lion, the ancient symbol of the Sinhala people, with orange and green stripes in the periphery representing the Tamils and the Muslims.

Hence the framing of Sri Lanka's constitutional crisis in terms of democracy is misleading. The resolution of the crisis will merely restore ethnocracy and provide the dominant ethnicity with the choice of electing a government.

As pointed out by Yiftachel and Ghanem, "Sri Lanka demonstrates the inability of an ethnocracy to be sustained for the long term, and its need to structurally reform in order to survive as a state."

Asia Times
7 March 2019

How Sri Lanka Wards off War Crimes Investigators

At the 40th session (February-March 2019) of the United Nations Human Rights Council (UNHRC), which began on February 25, Sri Lanka is expected show that it has complied with Resolution 30/1, which was passed during the 30th session (September-October 2015). Between March 2012 and March 2014, three resolutions were passed by the UNHRC calling on the Sri Lankan government to promote reconciliation, accountability and human rights. The main component of these resolutions called for an impartial international investigation into alleged war crimes committed during the final phase of the civil war.

However, at the 30th session, the UNHRC relaxed its call for an international inquiry by opting for a hybrid court that included both international and local judges and prosecutors to conduct the probe into war crimes. At the UNHRC's 34th Session in March 2017, the Sri Lankan government was allowed by way of Resolution 34/1 a period of two years to meet the requirements outlined in the 30/1 Resolution.

Duplicity, Delay and Defiance

Having vehemently opposed the resolutions passed between 2012 and 2014, the Sri Lankan government co-sponsored resolutions 30/1 and 34/1. This appeared to indicate a willingness to cooperate with the UN, signaling a change in the attitude of the new government under President Maithripala Sirisena, who had taken over from the hard-line Mahinda Rajapaksa in January 2015. Instead, it turned out to be part of a broader strategy to thwart any probe into alleged war crimes.

According to Human Rights Watch, despite government pledges, there has been little progress in prosecuting those responsible for wartime abuses or providing justice for victims.[1] This comes as no surprise in view of President Sirisena's declaration in November 2017, within seven months of co-sponsoring a resolution extending the probe by a further two years, that "There won't be electric chairs, international tribunals or foreign judges. That book is closed."[2]

On February 12, Prime Minister Ranil Wickremesinghe presented to cabinet a memorandum to establish a Truth and Reconciliation Commission, similar to what was established in post-apartheid South Africa. There was no mention of any probe into alleged war crimes. This was promptly condemned by former United Nations High Commissioner for Human Rights Navi Pillay, who was highly critical of the Sri Lankan government in an interview with Ceylon Today[3], saying:

"I am disappointed to learn that on the eve of the interactive dialogue on the Office of the United Nations High Commissioner for Human Rights'[OHCHR] report on Sri Lanka in the UN Human Rights Council, the government of Sri Lanka is resorting to yet another delaying tactic to escape......implementation of Resolution 30/L."

Ignoring Pillai's strong criticism, on February 16 nine days before the commencement of the UNHRC's 40th session, Prime Minister Wickramasinghe sealed the issue once and for all by calling on the Tamils to "forget the past and move forward"[4] implicitly dismissing any investigation into war crimes agreed under Resolution 30/1. Journalists for Democracy Sri Lanka (JDS)[5] pointed out that after four years of inaction to prosecute the armed forces accused of war crimes and crimes against humanity, Wickremesinghe had made it clear that the government has no intention of establishing accountability.

The Sri Lankan Prime Minister's actions were not surprising. Since co-sponsoring Resolution 30/1, Colombo has done little to implement the resolution. This was quite evident even by early last year.

Universal Jurisdiction

Therefore, it was not surprising that the then high commissioner for the UNHRC, Zeid Ra'ad Al-Hussein, should urge member states to explore other avenues to foster accountability in Sri Lanka, including the application of universal jurisdiction. Unfortunately, actions taken in pursuance of universal jurisdiction do not succeed where the alleged criminal enjoys diplomatic immunity. In Sri Lanka's case, many of the alleged war criminals are senior diplomats or enjoy immunity because of their high office. Indeed there were at least three instances where attempts to foster accountability through the application of universal jurisdiction[6] against alleged Sri Lankan war criminals failed.

Colombo's behavior since then has been deliberately provocative. In early 2019, Major General Shavendra Silva, an alleged war criminal, was appointed as chief of staff of the army. This was the man under whose command places designated as safe zones (no fire zones) and hospitals were deliberately bombed, resulting in the deaths of tens of thousands. Also, a large number of Tamil people, including infants and children under 10 years, who surrendered to the army division under Silva's direct command were never to be seen again and are now regarded as having "disappeared." The human rights organization International Truth & Justice Project (ITJP), which has focused its work on atrocities committed during the Sri Lankan civil war, called the appointment "a shocking new low for Sri Lanka"[7].

Although the UNHRC can pass resolutions, it has no mandate to implement resolutions or impose sanctions. At best, its resolutions are just recommendations.

Aware of this shortfall, the International Commission of Jurists (ICJ), an international non-governmental organization which promotes human rights and the rule of law, in its written submission[8] to the 40th Session of the UNHCR, argued that the gravity of the crimes committed and the failure to mete out justice fully warrants referral to the International Criminal Court or the creation of another international mechanism to facilitate criminal accountability. The ICJ's recommendations carry considerable weight as it is a standing group of 60 eminent jurists (including senior judges, attorneys and academics) with consultative status with the UN since 1957. Much will depend, however, on how the ICJ's argument is acted upon as the process requires the matter being referred to the UN's Security Council.

In the meantime, Sri Lanka has been successful in warding off any investigations into war crimes. Its strategy of duplicity, delay and defiance appears to have paid off.

The Diplomat
3 April 2019

The Geopolitics of Sri Lanka's Transitional Justice

Western countries are less interested in pressuring Sri Lanka now that Rajapaksa is no longer in charge.

On March 21, at the 40th Session of the United Nations Human Rights Council (UNHRC) Sri Lanka was granted another two-year extension to implement Resolution 30/1, "Promoting reconciliation, accountability and human rights in Sri Lanka." The resolution was originally passed on October 1, 2015, meaning the extension will give the Sri Lankan state almost six years to implement the resolution. Furthermore, unlike prior resolutions passed between March 2012 and March 2014, Resolution 30/1 did not insist on the probe into crimes committed during the civil war to be conducted by international investigators. Instead, it provided for a hybrid arrangement involving both international and local judges and prosecutors to participate in the investigations.

In the meantime, there has been hardly any pressure on Sri Lanka to meet its obligations. This was despite

President Maithripala Sirisena declaring on November 2017 that there won't be "international war crimes tribunals or foreign judges[1]," Prime Minister Ranil Wickremesinghe, on February 16, 2019, asking the Tamils to "forget the past and move forward[2]," and the Sri Lankan Foreign Minister Tilak Marapana[3], announcing on March 20, 2019 that the country's constitution does not allow foreign judges, dismissing the idea of a hybrid court, an integral part of Resolution 30/1.

It is plain that as far as the Sri Lankan government is concerned there is no intention to implement Resolution 30/1. More to the point, it appears even the states that backed the resolution are not serious about its implementation — a major shift in the approach pursued prior to January 2015.

This shift became evident in April 2016 when Samantha Power, then the U.S. representative to the United Nations, declared that Sri Lanka had, "since January 2015 emerged as a global champion of human rights and democratic accountability[4]" — this despite no progress being made by the Sri Lankan state to implement Resolution 30/1. In a similar vein, on January 28, 2019, ignoring the ongoing protests by the mothers of the disappeared, the continued militarization of the Tamil homeland in northern Sri Lanka, and the Sri Lankan army, navy, and air force continuing to occupy private land owned by civilians[5], the U.S. ambassador to Sri Lanka, Alaina B. Teplitz, tweeted that[6] "Celebrating differences while embracing a single national identity is a value the US & #LKA share."

Prior to October 2015, resolutions passed by the UNHRC were followed by pressure on Sri Lanka to implement these resolutions. For example, in November 2013, seven months after the UN had passed a resolution calling for independent investigations into alleged war crimes in Sri Lanka, then-Canadian Prime Minister Stephen Harper boycotted[7] the Commonwealth Heads of Government Meeting (CHOGM) held in Colombo, citing the absence of accountability by the host country for serious violations of international humanitarian standards during and after the civil war. Then-U.K. Prime Minister David Cameron attended CHOGM in Colombo but pressed for a credible investigation into alleged war crimes[8] and laid an ultimatum before the Sri Lankan government for a probe into the charges of human rights violations and war crimes. In December 2013, the United States warned Sri Lanka that the international community's "patience would start to wear thin" over Colombo's failure to investigate war crimes allegations[9]. Then in February 2014 Nisha Biswal[10], then the assistant secretary of state for South and Central Asia, during her visit to Sri Lanka, went onto express U.S. concerns about the worsening human rights situation.

In dealing with Sri Lanka's alleged war crimes, the approach pursued by the international actors prior to 2015 was thus markedly different to that pursued since

2015. The change clearly highlights the geopolitics behind the war crimes-related resolutions passed at the UNHRC since March 2012.

Until January 2015, Sri Lanka's president was Mahinda Rajapaksa, who had strengthened the Colombo-Beijing axis in return for China's assistance in crushing the Tamil rebellion. Wen Liao, chairwoman of the U.K. based Longford Advisors, pointed to this in an article aptly titled "China Crosses the Rubicon"[11],written within a month of Colombo's Beijing-assisted victory. According to her, for two decades China was guided by the concept of "peaceful rise," but "on Sri Lanka's beachfront battlefields, China's 'peaceful rise' was completed." Today, having gained a foothold in the strategically significant island of Sri Lanka, China seeks to shape the diplomatic agenda in order to increase China's options while constricting those of potential adversaries.

This did not go unnoticed by Washington. A December 2009, U.S. Senate Foreign Relations Committee report, "Sri Lanka: Re-charting U.S. Strategy after the War[12]," noted that Sri Lanka's "strategic drift" toward China "will have consequences for U.S. interests in the region." Declaring that "the United States cannot afford to 'lose' Sri Lanka," the report called for increasing "U.S. leverage vis-à-vis Sri Lanka" by adopting a multifaceted, broader and more robust approach to secure U.S. interests.

The opportunity to pursue such a policy presented itself

in March 2011 when a UN Panel of Experts appointed by the UN secretary general found "credible allegations[13]" that as many as 40,000 civilians may have been killed in the final months of the civil war, mostly as a result of indiscriminate shelling by the Sri Lankan military.

Armed with this report, the United States sponsored a resolution that was passed at the UNHRC in March 2012 calling on Colombo to address alleged abuses of international humanitarian law. In March 2013 and in March 2014, the UNHRC adopted similar resolutions calling on Sri Lanka to undertake a comprehensive investigation into alleged violations and abuses of human rights and related crimes.

In late November 2014, there was an unexpected development when one of Rajapaksa's senior ministers, Maithripala Sirisena, resigned his position to run against Rajapaksa in the presidential election to be held in January 2015. The West-leaning United National Party (UNP) endorsed Sirisena as a "common candidate," further undermining Rajapaksa's attempt to seek an unprecedented third term in office. Sirisena won the presidential elections and promptly appointed Wickremesinghe, the leader of the UNP, as the country's prime minister.

With a West-leaning prime minister in office, and the China-friendly Rajapaksa gone, Washington began to ease its tough stand on Sri Lanka's alleged war crimes. The first indications came when Sri Lanka sought and obtained Washington's help to postpone the release of an UNHRC report on Sri Lankan war crimes from March to September 2015. At the September/October UNHRC hearings on Sri Lanka's alleged war crimes, the United States secured an extension of two years for Sri Lanka to implement the UNHRC Resolution passed on that occasion (Resolution 30/1), which called for the investigations to be undertaken by a hybrid court instead of an independent international court unlike the previous resolutions. In March 2019, when Sri Lanka was found to have made little progress, a further extension of two years was provided.

Apparently, as long Sri Lanka's government leans toward the West, the "stick" has been abandoned in favor of the "carrot," underscoring the geopolitics that underpin calls for accountability over Sri Lanka's war crimes.

Asia Times
21 June 2019

Sri Lanka's Muslims Bloodied by Buddhism

Sri Lanka has become more fragile, fractured and polarized following the Easter Sunday bomb attacks as the country's Muslims are harassed and subjected to violence by mobs of Sinhala Buddhists who form the majority of the island's population.

Although those targeted by jihadist violence on Easter Sunday were the island's Christians, it has been Sinhala Buddhist mobs led by saffron-clad Buddhist monks that have been at the forefront of the ongoing attacks against Muslims. The Easter Sunday atrocities have simply served as a convenient excuse to revive the anti-Muslim violence that plagued the island in 2014 and again in 2018.

State-Condoned anti-Muslim Violence

In the wake of the Easter Sunday carnage, hundreds of Muslims have been arrested[1] under the Prevention of Terrorism Act, which gives sweeping powers to the police to arrest and detain civilians without a warrant or evidence. On May 23, the Sri Lankan newspaper *Divaina,*[2] known for its pro-Sinhala Buddhist nationalist stance, published a front-page article alleging that a Muslim doctor secretly sterilized 4,000 Sinhala Buddhist women. Two days later, despite the absence of any evidence to support this wild allegation, the doctor, Segu Shihabdeen Mohamed Shafi, was arrested. The police then took the unusual step of calling for evidence after the arrest.

The executive director of the International Centre for Ethnic Studies (ICES), Mario Gomez, fears that such actions by state forces will lead to the radicalization of Muslims.[3]

Events certainly have gained a momentum of their own with several Muslim properties being destroyed by marauding mobs.

In late May, a Buddhist monk, Athuraliye Rathana Thero, called for the two Muslim provincial governors and a Muslim government minister to be sacked on the unsubstantiated grounds that they were linked to the Easter Sunday carnage. Another Buddhist monk, Galagoda Aththe Gnanasara,[4] head of the hardline Bodu Bala Sena (BBS), or "Buddhist Power Force," threatened to escalate the protests if these men were not sacked.

For the first time, the Muslim leadership acted decisively – all government ministers and the two provincial governors handed in their resignations in protest. Rauff Hakim,[5] a senior member of the cabinet and leader of the Sri Lankan Muslim Congress (SLMM), a partner of the government, was forthright in articulating that the action was taken in order to not capitulate to xenophobic forces and force the government to contain them. What was unsaid was that the government of which he was part was complicit in allowing anti-Muslim violence to continue. It was clear that the mobs had the support of high-ranking government officials, members of the police and security forces who had turned a blind eye when the mobs were attacking Muslim property – mosques, homes and shops.

The state's complicity became blindingly obvious when In the midst of the ongoing anti-Muslim violence, Galagoda Aththe Gnanasara Thero, the head of BBS, who had been imprisoned for six years for contempt of court, was pardoned by Sri Lanka's president on May 23 and allowed to continue with his hate speeches instigating anti-Muslim violence.

On June 18, the prelate of the Asgiriya Chapter, Warakagoda Sri Gnanarathana, upped the ante by calling for the stoning of Muslims and the boycotting of Muslim-owned shops. Anti-Muslim violence has now been officially sanctioned by no less than the head of the Asgiriya Chapter, one of the two most influential Buddhist orders in Sri Lanka.

Sinhala Buddhist Hegemony

Rauff Hakim's demand that xenophobic forces be

contained is unlikely to be heeded as giving into "minority demands" will only strengthen the hands of the opposition. This is because Sri Lanka's post-colonial history has been shaped by an ideology that seeks to promote Sinhala Buddhist hegemony and any party seen to be "soft" in upholding this ideal is at a disadvantage in the next elections. With the Asgiria prelate's order in place, the government is unlikely to take any measure to contain anti-Muslim sentiments or actions.

Between independence in 1948 and July 1983, mob violence was frequently unleashed against the Tamils of the island to contain their demand for self-rule as this was thought to undermine Sinhala Buddhist hegemony. More to the point, any sitting government's effort to seek accommodation with the Tamils was seized by the opposition as a sell-out, a move actively supported by the Buddhist clergy. The unprecedented level of violence unleashed in July 1983, since known as Black July, resulted in a mass Tamil uprising, plunging the country into a civil war that was put down with genocidal brutality 26 years later.

Muslim Response to Sinhala Buddhist Hegemony

Sri Lanka's Muslims, although disadvantaged by the Sinhala Buddhist hegemony that was integral to Sri Lanka's majoritarian rule, sought to manage the situation not by demanding rights but by joining both major political parties and obtaining concessions for their community. This was an acceptable arrangement for both Sinhala-dominated political parties, the center-left Sri Lanka Freedom Party (SLFP) and the right-leaning United National Party (UNP). The Muslim leaders delivered Muslim votes en bloc to their parties and were, in turn, offered positions in government. Later on, this en bloc vote was delivered not along party lines but largely through a party of their own, the Sri Lanka Muslim Congress (SLMM). The SLMM helped form a government by joining the party that was likely to provide the most benefits. The SLMM was not constrained by leftist, centrist or rightist ideology. During the war between the Sri Lankan state and the Tamil people, the Muslim community, although Tamil-speaking, took a position in line with the Sinhala-dominated state. This strategy helped the community survive the war and even prosper.

Despite the Muslim community's non-confrontational, subservient and ingratiating approach, it had earned the wrath of Sinhala Buddhist nationalists, who believed that this community had also become a threat to Sinhala Buddhist supremacy on the island.

Buddhist Triumphalism

Whereas the Sri Lankan state's anti-Tamil actions, both legislative and administrative, were based on the notion that they were disproportionately represented in the public service and universities, the anti-Muslim sentiments are the product of a premise that Muslim population growth is much greater than that of the Sinhala Buddhists and could erode Sinhala Buddhist hegemony. Additionally, it is believed that Muslims hold more economic power than is warranted by their population, that they are trying to convert people, and that they are an alien group that has not integrated with mainstream Sri Lanka.

Perhaps the best explanation for the anti-Muslim sentiments since 2014, five years after the Tamil rebellion was put down, is triumphalism. The victory over the Tamils appears to have given the Sinhala Buddhist hardliners the impetus to subjugate another non-Sinhala Buddhist group and re-assert Sinhala Buddhist hegemony.

Driven by notions of hegemony, apprehension and triumphalism, Sri Lanka's Buddhists may resort to further violence pushing the Muslims into violence of their own that may well break up the already fragile polity that Sri Lanka is.

The Diplomat
2 August 2019

US Push for New Military Agreement Runs into Fierce Opposition in Sri Lanka

Negotiations over a renewed Status of Forces Agreement sparked local concerns about a possible U.S. base.

In view of its strategic location in the Indian Ocean, Sri Lanka is of interest to both Washington and Beijing as they seek to increase their presence in the Indian Ocean.[1] Washington's latest attempt to improve its position in Sri Lanka involves renegotiating the Status of Forces Agreement (SOFA) originally signed in mid-1995 when Beijing was not on the scene.

However, opposition to the renewed SOFA within Sri Lanka has been intense on the grounds that it would involve establishing U.S. bases in the island and thus compromise the country's sovereignty. Indeed, U.S. Secretary of State Mike Pompeo's decision to cancel his visit to Colombo on June 27 has been attributed to rising local opposition[2] against the signing of SOFA. Sri Lankan President Maithripala Sirisena, who heads the centrist Sri Lanka Freedom Party (SLFP), has been forthright in ruling out the presence of any American troops or base on the island. Sri Lankan Army Commander Mahesh Senanayake is similarly inclined, telling local media that he would not sign the SOFA.[3] Sri Lankan Defense Secretary Gen (Rtd) Shantha Kottegoda[4] also objected to the SOFA, saying that foreign troops were not needed in Sri Lanka. Opposition to SOFA has also been expressed by Mahajana Eksath Peramuna (MEP), an Sinhala ultra-nationalist party closely aligned to Rajapaksa-led Sri Lanka People's Party (SLPP) and the Marxist Janatha Vimukthi Peramuna (JVP).

Prime Minister Ranil Wickremesinghe, who heads the right-leaning United National Party (UNP) that enjoys a majority in parliament, is responsible for renegotiating the SOFA. On July 10, Wickremesinghe told parliament that the proposed SOFA "was not a military pact'[5] but only an agreement establishing the rights and privileges that U.S. military personnel would enjoy if they were in the country," according to *Reuters*. "The SOFA is a peacetime document,"[6] he said. Wickremesinghe then went onto reassure parliament he would not support any agreement that threatens Sri Lanka's sovereignty.

However, according to a leaked version of the SOFA obtained by Sri Lanka's *Sunday Times* on June 30, the agreement would permit the free movement and passage of U.S. military personnel, vessels and aircraft in the country.[7] *Sunday Times* drew attention to a clause in the leaked document waiving criminal jurisdiction over U.S. personnel while in Sri Lanka, causing particularly strong criticism.

In an attempt to allay fears about SOFA, the U.S. Mission in Sri Lanka has begun to refer to the proposed agreement as a Visiting Forces Agreement (VFA) giving it a much softer tone by underplaying the notion of U.S. forces becoming a permanent feature in the island's political landscape. Pushing this line, U.S. Ambassador Alaina Teplitz told the local media that the proposed agreement was primarily designed to address a number of red tape issues. She insisted the United States had "no plan or intention to establish a US base in Sri Lanka.[8] But many in Sri Lanka found it hard to swallow her claim that China is not the motivating factor behind U.S. interest in a military agreement Sri Lanka.[9] It is a common belief among Sri Lanka's political players and analysts that U.S. interest in Sri Lanka is predicated on the December 2009 U.S. Senate Foreign Relations Committee report, "Sri Lanka: Re-charting US Strategy after the War." That report noted that the United States cannot afford to "lose" Sri Lanka to China. There is no indication that this approach has changed under the current Trump administration.

Also, Teplitz, in her attempt to address concerns about U.S. soldiers enjoying immunity for offenses committed in Sri Lanka, implied[10] that arrangements would be in place for U.S. soldiers to be tried by U.S. courts should they breach any law just like Sri Lankan soldiers accused of crimes overseas were subject to trial in Sri Lankan courts. If she meant this to reassure, it was a bad example. Sri Lanka has never prosecuted a single soldier for sexual misconduct[11] while serving in a peacekeeping mission abroad in Haiti, despite over 100 being accused of running a child sex ring. Thus the U.S. ambassador had only managed to deepen suspicions that U.S. soldiers too may be able to get away with crimes.

Caught between the mounting hysteria about the SOFA and the ambassador's unhelpful remarks, Wickremesinghe is finding it hard to convince his detractors. As a result the renegotiation of SOFA appears to have run into trouble. However, given Colombo's significance in the U.S. Indo-Pacific Strategy the United States is unlikely to give up.

Asia Times
8 August 2019

What Colombo-Beijing Axis Means to Sri Lanka

While the ongoing attempt by the US to renegotiate the Status of Forces Agreement (SOFA) has run into fierce opposition[1] the gift of a 2,300-tonne warship by Beijing to Colombo in early July this year has been warmly welcomed by Sri Lanka's authorities. The commander of the Sri Lankan Navy, Vice Admiral Piyal De Silva, thanked China[2] for the frigate and proclaimed it to be a sign of the good friendship between the two countries. According to China's mission in Colombo, 110 Sri Lankan Navy personnel spent two months in Shanghai being trained how to operate the ship.

Later the same month, Reuters[3] reported that Chinese President Xi Jinping offered Sri Lanka a fresh grant of 2 billion yuan ($295 million), a clear indication that Beijing is looking to further expand its influence over Colombo. Surprisingly, this has not caused any outcry, although it is well known that Beijing, through an adroit combination of grants, bribes[4] and "debt trap diplomacy,"[5] has successfully encroached on Sri Lanka's sovereignty. Instead, Sri Lanka's nationalists, (a euphemism that best describes Sinhala nationalists) consider themselves indebted to China for helping crush the 30-year old Tamil rebellion. It is a matter of fact that if not for the help of the Chinese, who, in addition to their military aid, gave the Sri Lankan government diplomatic cover[6] at the UN Security Council, Colombo could not have won the long-running civil war.

The Colombo-Beijing axis is primarily driven by Sri Lanka's nationalists to counter their real or imagined threat from New Delhi.

As a consequence, Sri Lanka's nationalists are grateful to China for its enormous help in bringing to an end what was widely regarded as an "unwinnable war," and are unable to regard Chinese actions as inimical to Sri Lanka's interests or impinge on Sri Lanka's sovereignty. This, despite Sri Lanka having been forced to lease out Hambantota port in the south for a period of 99 years (to be managed and operated by Chinese state-owned China Merchants Ports Holdings) and China openly seeking to derail the Sri Lankan government's agreement with Japan and India for the development of the Easter Container Terminal (ECT).

Instead, Sri Lanka's nationalists are inclined to look upon Washington's outright grant of $480 million over a five -year period[7] in conjunction with the renegotiation of the SOFA agreement and negotiations for the Acquisition and Cross Servicing Agreement (ACSA) as the country becoming "one of the territories of the USA, if not its 51st State."[8] Unfortunately, such hysterical and outrageous hyperbole appear to be typical of Sri

Lanka's nationalists.

The explanation for this apparent irrational loyalty to China is attributable to the well-established premise that Sri Lanka's Sinhala nationalists are a "majority with a minority complex."[9] As such they entertain the fear that the Tamils of Sri Lanka, with the support of the huge Tamil population across the Palk Straits in the southern Indian state of Tamil Nadu, may prove to be a threat to their own independence or even cause the Tamil homeland in the northeast to be annexed by India.

Hence, the blind, unthinking loyalty to China by Sri Lankan nationalists in whose view China was not only the only country that had helped them beat Sri Lanka's Tamils into submission, but also the country that has the military and diplomatic might to counter India should it prove to be a threat.

Sinhala nationalists, that is, the overwhelming majority within the Sinhala population, fear India because they believe that on the long term, New Delhi, either due to pressure from the southern Indian state of Tamil Nadu, which is angered by Sri Lanka's ongoing mistreatment of their vanquished fellow Tamils, or to gain access to Sri Lanka's port of Trincomalee, which New Delhi is known to covet, may directly intervene.

The Colombo-Beijing axis is primarily driven by Sri Lanka's nationalists to counter their real or imagined threat from New Delhi. The opposition to Washington is a corollary, because Washington's policy calls for a robust approach to break up the Colombo-Beijing axis and improve its own influence over Colombo.

Sri Lanka's Victor's Peace and the Way Forward

Just before the Sri Lankan state defeated the Tamil rebel forces, Professor Damien Kingsbury of Australia's Deakin University, wrote that without a political agreement to address the grievances of Sri Lanka's Tamils, it is likely that Sri Lanka will continue to be beset by a different, and perhaps more intractable, type of conflict.[1]

A Victor's Peace

A decade later, as foreseen by Professor Kingsbury, the conflict has become intractable as a direct consequence of the Sinhala leadership, buoyed by its triumph, choosing to maintain the *status quo*. Thus the 'peace' that ensued has been a Victor's Peace.

In 2013, four years after having won the war against the Tamil rebels, the then Defence Secretary and current Presidential aspirant Gotabaya Rajapaksa declared Sri Lanka to be one of the peaceful, stable and democratically secured countries in the world.[2] Seven years later, *News First*[3], a Colombo based news media outlet jubilantly announced, on 19 May

2019 that marked the 10th anniversary of the end of the war, as the "Decade of Peace". On 21 April 2019, Colombo's *Reuters*[4] correspondent, subscribing to the same notion, reported the killing of over 250 people on Easter Sunday by an Islamic fundamentalist group as having shattered almost "ten years of peace".

Notwithstanding these positions taken by sections of the Colombo establishment, it is impossible to deny that the violence over three decades was the product of a persistent refusal by the Sri Lankan state to address the root cause, i.e. Sri Lanka's unitary constitution, based on a 'control model' where the majority segment dominates and reduces all other segments to a position of subordination.[5]

Hence, what passes for peace in Sri Lanka is a 'negative peace' or the absence of overt conflict.[6] Unlike a harmonious peace, a negative peace needs to be enforced literally at the point of a gun. This explains the heavy military presence in the Tamil provinces where military personnel to civilians is reported to be sitting at a 1:5 ratio.[7]

The Failure of the Politics of Persuasion

When the war was brought to an end with the demise of the Liberation Tigers of Tamil Eelam (LTTE) , the mantle of Tamil leadership came to reside with the Tamil National Alliance (TNA). Acutely aware of the absence of a countervailing force in the form of the

LTTE and not sufficiently informed to take advantage of the geopolitics that offered some opportunities to strengthen their bargaining capabilities, TNA adopted a pragmatic approach to deal with the Sri Lankan Government. Assuming that the Sri Lanka Government is likely to concede 'little' rather than more TNA, framed its demand within the concept of shared sovereignty coupled with a gradualist approach to improve on its minimalist demands. TNA's ultimate aim was a form of federalism that entailed some form of self-rule for the Tamil region. It was inclined to rely on the goodwill of New Delhi and the Washington-led West to realise its goals.TNA also appears to have placed its trust on assurances provided by Sinhalese leaders, paying little heed to history. Not surprisingly, this approach has not worked. Frustrated, TNA's R Sampanthan, speaking at the 16th National Convention of the TNA on June 30, 2019, asserted the need to think about an armed struggle.[8] It does not take much to realise it was just rhetoric by an aging politician, who had lost all credibility to gain some political attention.

International Dimensions

While, Beijing has a significant presence in Sri Lanka, New Delhi's influence is limited. Washington is focused on gaining a foothold in the island. Should Washington regard that it is perceived by the Sri Lankan state as being supportive of the Tamils, Washington, will have no qualms about abandoning its support (if any) to the Tamil people. When the pro-Beijing Rajapaksas were in power, the US anxious to weaken the Colombo-Beijing axis called for increasing US leverage vis-à-vis Sri Lanka by adopting a multifaceted, broader and robust approach[9]. This included calling for a political solution to the conflict and being highly critical of the Rajapaksa regime. But following the 'regime change' that resulted in Rajapaksa being displaced by Sirisena and more importantly the pro-Washington Ranil Wickramasinghe ensconced as Prime Minister, US' enthusiasm to promote a political solution has considerably waned .

As long as the Sri Lankan state remains intransigent about sharing political power through an arrangement based on a federal union, Sri Lanka's problem will not only become more intractable but will become fertile grounds for foreign actors to exploit the ongoing conflict to their own advantage, whereas a genuine political arrangement underpinned by a federal constitution providing self-rule for the Tamil people will benefit the island as a whole.

Peace Dividends

A stable peace is bound to yield dividends.

These 'peace dividends' would invariably include investments by the Tamil diaspora; investments by foreign investors; the elimination of unproductive public expenditure incurred on imposing a Victor's Peace and a Sri Lanka freed from the shackles of internal conflict being able to leverage the competing interests of foreign powers to its advantage.

Responsibility Lies with the Sinhala People

Bringing about peace is easier said than done. And in respect of an 'internal' conflict, a daunting challenge. The writer is therefore inclined to use the analogy of resolving domestic violence where the parties for whatever reasons are not able to separate. The domestic violence analogy is not new, it has in fact been used before by the late Mr S Sivanayagam, former editor of the *Saturday Review* to explain the armed response by the Tamil militants to that of an abused wife wielding a knife in desperation.

In situations of domestic violence, the latest research has established that responsibility to change lies with the initial perpetrators of violence-men in the majority of the cases. This is not surprising because in all societies, the power dynamics favour men. The change, however, will have to be made by the perpetrator, more importantly their peers and other men who are in a position to influence the perpetrators to end their violence. It stands to commonsense that the victims of violence can in any event be in a position to resolve the situation, short of separating.

Extending this analogy to the 'internal 'conflict in Sri Lanka, the responsibility to bring about a meaningful political change resides not with the Tamil people, but with the Sinhala people. And it is not just the politicians who have carried out the violence who are responsible for this change, but all Sinhala people committed to peace. It is they who can influence their fellow Sinhalese who can then influence their politicians.

This, I believe is the way forward should Sri Lanka wish to replaces its Victor's Peace with a harmonious peace that will enable peaceful coexistence.

(Endnotes)

The International Dimensions of the Conflict in Sri Lanka

1   Lunstead J in " The United State's role in Sri Lanka's Peace Process 2002-2006" originally published by The Asia Foundation in 2007 and included in the CJPD's Publication 'International Dimensions of the Conflict in Sri Lanka", 2008

2   Das R N. "China's Foray into Sri Lanka and India's Response" http://www.idsa.in/idsacomments/ChinasForayintoSriLankaandIndiasResponse_rndas_050810

3   Reuters, "UN rights body backs Sri Lankan resolution on war", 27 May 2009, http://www.alertnet.org/thenews/newsdesk/LR170562.htm

4   Rajasingham AT , "Shocking revelation of what Fonseka did in U S", Asian Tribune ,14 February 2010 "http://www.asiantribune.com/news/2010/02/14/shocking-revelation-what-fonseka-did-u-s-asian-tribune

5   Das R N. "China's Foray into Sri Lanka and India's Response"

http://www.idsa.in/idsacomments/
ChinasForayintoSriLankaandIndiasResponse_
rndas_050810 (website of the Indian Institute for
Defence studies and Analysis (IDSA).

6   Ramu Manivannan, "Historical Shift - India, Sri
Lanka and the Tamils" 7 June 2010 http://www.
southasiaanalysis.org/papers39/paper3847.html
(website of the South Asia Analysis Group).

7   Saibal Das Gupta "China calls PoK 'northern
Pakistan', J&K is 'India-controlled Kashmir'"
Times of India 2 September 2010

8   Wall Street Journal Asian Edition "The Chinese
Military Challenge" 18 August 2010

9   Bill Gertz,"China removed as top priority for
spies", Washington Times 20 August 2010

10   Ibid

11   William R. Hawkins," Why Did U.S. Kowtow to
Chinese Naval Ambitions?", Accuracy in Media,
27 July 2010 http://www.aim.org/guest-column/
why-did-u-s-kowtow-to-chinese-naval-ambitions/

12   Jacques M, "When China Rules the World: The
Rise of the Middle Kingdom and the End of the
Western World "Allen Lane, UK 2009,p340

13   Wen Liao , "China Crosses the Rubicon",
     Financial Review, 23 June 2009

14   ibid

Sri Lanka: In the Eye of the Storm

1   Wen Liao in "China Crosses the Rubicon",
     Australian Financial Review,23rd June 2009

2   South Asia's Unheralded Stories in: http://www.
     state.gov/p/sca/rls/rmks/2010/148505.htm#

Required: A Sri Lanka Policy

1   The article was published by South Asian
     analysis Group under the title "Required: A Sri
     Lanka Policy - An Expat Sri Lankan Tamil's
     view". This was misleading as the writer was not
     an expatriate Sri Lankan Tamil but an Australian
     national of Sri Lankan Tamil decent and hence
     the change to the title.

2   A Pratap in "Lessons to be learnt from the rout of
     the LTTE" –The Week 31 May 2009

3   The International Crisis Group "India and Sri
     Lanka after the LTTE", June 2011, p6

4   Ibid p4-5

5   Mohan Ram, Sri Lanka: The Fractured Island, New Delhi: Penguin Books (India), 1989,p138

6   Ethnic flooding – the continuing and deliberate settling of Sinhalese populations on land in the Tamil homeland – to alter the demographic balance and thereby systemically erase the Tamil nation's territorial identity- S Sathanathan in "After Pirapakaran: Deepening Internal Colonialism", http://www.sangam.org/2010/08/Internal_Colonialism.php,.

7   D T Hagerty,"India's Regional Security Doctrine", Asian Survey, Vol: XXXXI, No 4, April 1991

8   S Rajappa, "India and 'the Killing Fields of Sri Lanka", The Statesman, 12 July 2011, http://thestatesman.net/index.php?option=com_content&view=article&id=376293&catid=38

9   http://www.ndtv.com/article/india/tamil-nadu-seeks-economic-sanctions-against-sri-lanka-/

10   Sumantra Bose is Professor of International and Comparative Politics at the London School of Economics and Political Science (LSE).

11   Jointly hosted by TRANCEND International and the Centre for Just Peace and Democracy (CJPD) in Switzerland in June 2007

12   S Bose, "India" in " International Dimensions
      of the Conflict in Sri Lanka" Centre for Just
      Peace and Democracy (CJPD) , Emmenbrucke,
      Switzerland, 2008.

Colombo's Military Build-Up:
A Strategy of Deterrence

1   https://thediplomat.com/2015/11/outwitting-pakistan-
      india-offers-sri-lanka-its-newest-fighter-jet/

2   https://asiancorrespondent.com/2015/06/sri-
      lanka-political-detainees/#1h06rTdmave35ftc.97

3   http://www.salem-news.com/articles/july162011/
      statesman-tamils-.php

4   https://www.theatlantic.com/magazine/
      archive/2009/07/to-catch-a-tiger/307581/

5   http://www.crisisgroup.org/~/media/Files/asia/
      south-asia/sri-lanka/206 India and Sri Lanka
      after the LTTE.pdf

Sri Lanka's Re-embrace of China Leaves
India out in the Cold

1   http://www.ceylontoday.lk/
      print20161101CT20161231.php?id=10492

2   https://www.project-syndicate.org/commentary/
      china-crosses-the-rubicon?barrier=true

3   https://www.gpo.gov/fdsys/pkg/CPRT-
     111SPRT53866/html/CPRT-111SPRT53866.htm

4   https://www.hrw.org/world-report/2015/
     country-chapters/sri-lanka

5   http://thediplomat.com/2015/12/renewed-us-sri-
     lanka-relations-a-slobbering-love-affair/

6   http://articles.economictimes.indiatimes.
     com/2016-04-10/news/72209850_1_
     hambantota-port-maritime-silk-road-
     wickremesinghe

7   http://www.shanghaidaily.com/article/article_
     xinhua.aspx?id=328035

8   E:\There was no question of pulling out when
     there was no summit to attend",

9   http://uswww.rediff.com/news/column/why-sri-
     lankas-need-for-china-will-continue/20150119.htm

10   http://www.dnaindia.com/india/report-brics-
     summit-2016-pm-modi-holds-bilateral-talks-
     with-lankan-president-sirisena-2264853

11   http://indianexpress.com/article/india/india-
     news-india/foreign-secretary-jaishankar-meets-
     lankan-president-sirisena-in-colombo-discusses-
     economic-collaboration-3098710/

12   http://www.thesundayleader.lk/2016/11/06/
     diplomatic-faux-pas-by-chinese-envoy-irks-
     government/

13   http://timesofindia.indiatimes.com/india/Debt-
     ridden-Sri-Lanka-snuggles-up-to-China-again-
     at-Indias-expense/articleshow/52056405.cms

The Tamil Nadu Factor:
Demanding Justice for Genocide in Sri Lanka

1   http://indianexpress.com/article/india/india-
     will-go-with-consensus-on-sri-lanka-resolution-
     at-unhrc-govt-4582476/

2   http://www.newindianexpress.com/states/
     tamil-nadu/2017/mar/20/aiadmk-wants-india-
     to-oppose-unhrc-resolution-on-sri-lankan-
     tamils-1583543.html

3   https://www.pressreader.com/india/
     the-hindu/20170318/28164248498667

4   http://www.thehindu.com/news/national/
     Tamil-Nadu-politics-on-the-cusp-of-change/
     article16769660.ece

5   http://sangam.org/2011/07/India_Killing_Fields.
     php?uid=4388

6   http://archive.boston.com/bostonglobe/
      editorial_opinion/oped/articles/2009/02/15/
      genocide_in_sri_lanka/

Extension Given to Probe Sri Lanka's War Crimes is No Surprise

1   https://www.opendemocracy.net/mark-salter/
      is-us-backtracking-on-sri-lankas-post-war-
      accountability-process

2   http://thediplomat.com/2016/04/samantha-
      power-misses-the-mark-on-sri-lanka-again/

3   http://www.aljazeera.com/programmes/
      talktojazeera/2016/01/sri-lankan-president-
      allegations-war-crimes-160128150748006.html

4   https://www.colombotelegraph.com/index.php/
      cbk-drops-bombshell-says-no-need-for-war-
      crimes-probe/

The Politics of Persuasion-An Evaluation

1   https://www.crisisgroup.org/asia/south-asia/
      sri-lanka/286-sri-lanka-s-transition-nowhere

2   Mark P Whitaker, "Learning Politics from
      Sivaram" Pluto Press, 2007,p190

3   Luxshi Vimalarajah and R Cheran, "Empowering Diasporas: The Dynamics of Post-War Transnational Politics", Berghof Peace Support, 2010,p28

4   Nadesan Satyendra,"Thirteenth Amendment to Sri Lanka Constitution, Governor, Chief Minster and Provincial Council-Devolution or Comic Opera "The London Tamil Forum, circa 1988,p4

5   Personal communication Gajendrakumar Ponnambalam, leader of the Tamil National People's Front, 2011

6   "TNPF leader speaks on independent, concerted Tamil foreign policy", *Tamilnet. com,* https://www.tamilnet.com/art. html?catid=79&artid=37355

7   http://www.omlanka.net/news/top-stories/842-sampanthan-sheds-light-on-tna-s-participation-at-independence-day-celebrations.html_

8   Vigneswaran Kajeepan, (9 June 2015). *Kajenthirakumar VS Sumanthiran.* Retrieved from https://www.youtube.com/ watch?v=-0TK8xjntOc

9   http://www.thehindu.com/news/international/ new-constitution-needed-tna/article7471412.ece

10   Thimpu principles or Thimpu Declaration
      were a set of four demands put forward by
      the Sri Lankan Tamil delegation at the Indian
      government organised peace talks in Thimpu,
      Bhutan in 1985. These four demands were the
      recognition of the Tamils of Ceylon as a nation;
      the existence of an identified homeland for the
      Tamils of Ceylon; the right of self-determination
      of the Tamil nation and the right to citizenship
      and the fundamental rights of all Tamils of
      Ceylon.

11   "TNA's Election Manifesto goes beyond Thimpu
      Principles M A Sumanthiran", (Translated
      from Tamil) http://www.globaltamilnews.
      net/GTMNEditorial/tabid/71/articleType/
      ArticleView/articleId/122692/language/en-US/

12   http://www.ceylonews.com/2016/11/tna-warns-
      colombo-not-to-take-its-conciliatory-approach-
      as-weakness-video/

13   Saman Gunesekera, "Unprecedented military
      budget in Sri Lanka",19 October 2012, *World
      Socialist Website* http://www.wsws.org/en/
      articles/2012/10/slec-019.html

14   "The Forever War?: Military Control in Sri
      Lanka's North" Crisis Group, 25 March 2014,
      http://blog.crisisgroup.org/asia/2014/03/25/the-
      forever-war-military-control-in-sri-lankas-north/

15   Stewart Motha, "Australia is playing a
      dangerous game with Sri Lanka", *The
      Guardian*, 21 February 2013, http://www.
      theguardian.com/commentisfree/2013/feb/21/
      australia-playing-dangerous-game-sri-lanka

16   Meera Srinivasan, TN politicians exploiting
      Lankan Tamils issue: C.V. Wigneswaran, Hindu,
      12 September 2013 http://www.thehindu.com/
      news/international/south-asia/tn-politicians-
      exploiting-lankan-tamils-issue-cv-wigneswaran/
      article5121012.ece

17   P Percival, "Tamil Proverbs with their English
      Translation", Dinavartamani Press, Mylapore,
      1874,p516

Sri Lanka: Sovereignty Compromised

1   https://www.colombotelegraph.com/index.php/
      indian-ocean-sri-lankas-role-in-determining-
      the-future-of-the-world/

2   https://www.forbes.com/sites/
      wadeshepard/2016/05/28/the-story-behind-the-
      worlds-emptiest-international-airport-sri-lankas-
      mattala-rajapaksa/#688a812f7cea

3   https://www.forbes.com/sites/
      wadeshepard/2017/08/14/india-to-sri-
      lanka-forget-china-we-want-your-empty-
      airport/#78e389e11ece

4   https://www.marinelink.com/news/
     resolve-salvage-removes343563

5   http://carnegieindia.org/2017/02/17/
     trincomalee-consultations-event-5532

6   http://www.thehindu.com/news/national/sri-
     lankan-pm-to-visit-india/article18161668.ece

7   http://indianexpress.com/article/india/pm-narendra-
     modi-to-visit-sri-lanka-in-may-4621978/

Trincomalee Beckons:
Is New Delhi Becoming Assertive?

1   https://timesofindia.indiatimes.com/india/Debt-
     ridden-Sri-Lanka-snuggles-up-to-China-again-
     at-Indias-expense/articleshow/52056405.cms

2   http://www.ft.lk/article/608598/Dr--Shashi-
     Tharoor-talks-India-way-for-Sri-Lanka

3   http://carnegieindia.org/2017/02/17/
     trincomalee-consultations-event-5532

4   https://www.thehindu.com/news/national/sri-
     lankan-pm-to-visit-india/article18161668.ece

5   https://indianexpress.com/article/india/
     pm-narendra-modi-to-visit-sri-lanka-in-
     may-4621978/

Realpolitik Not Humanitarian Concerns
Will Decide Myanmar's Future

1   http://www.atimes.com/
geopolitics-will-decide-fate-rohingya/

2   https://www.washingtonpost.com/graphics/2017/
world/rohingya/?utm_term=.bdd99cf4ce35

3   https://www.einpresswire.com/
article/336403654/black-july-we-remember-
july-1983-which-birthed-institutionalization-of-
sinhala-militarized-oppression-of-tamils-tgte

4   ibid

5   https://thediplomat.com/2017/09/
sri-lanka-sovereignty-compromised/

6   http://www.business-standard.com/article/
economy-policy/india-s-response-to-the-
rohingya-crisis-is-driven-by-an-un-fine-
balance-117091800136_1.html

7   http://www.theaustralian.com.au/news/world/
china-backs-myanmars-attacks-on-rohingyas/
news-story/df4d46525a42eed0a466782

8   http://edition.cnn.com/2017/09/08/politics/
us-myanmar-rohingya/index.html

9   http://www.newsweek.com/myanmarrohingya-muslimsfleeing-myanmarisis-recruitmentsoutheast-asiarohingya-604185

10   http://www.southasiaanalysis.org/node/2159

Sri Lankan Constitution: The Strategy of Doublespeak

1   http://dailynews.lk/2017/07/12/local/121719/unitary-state-buddhism-will-be-upheld-new-constitution-president

2   https://www.newsradio.lk/2017/09/21/new-constitution-calls-unitary-state-pm/

Sri Lanka's Proposed Constitution Comes Under Attack

1   https://www.colombotelegraph.com/index.php/supporters-of-new-constitution-must-be-killed-major-general-kamal-gunaratne/

2   https://www.colombotelegraph.com/index.php/the-federalisation-plot-the-proof/

3   https://www.colombotelegraph.com/index.php/new-constitution-what-we-expect-from-the-two-main-parties/

4   https://www.colombotelegraph.com/index.php/
sinhalese-wont-give-anything-we-must-try-to-
obtain-our-rights-under-international-laws-
wigneswaran/

India's Regional Power Credentials under Threat by China

1   https://timesofindia.indiatimes.com/india/china-
role-in-indian-ocean-region-india-discusses-
maldives-turmoil-with-us/articleshow/61514665.cms

2   https://timesofindia.indiatimes.com/india/china-
role-in-indian-ocean-region-india-discusses-
maldives-turmoil-with-us/articleshow/61514565.
cms

3   http://indianexpress.com/article/india/
maldives-must-be-mindful-of-indias-security-
in-indian-ocean-former-president-mohamed-
nasheed-4760337/

4   http://m.koreatimes.co.kr/phone/news/view.
jsp?req_newsidx=47506

5   https://www.crisisgroup.org/asia/south-asia/
india-non-kashmir/india-and-sri-lanka-after-ltte

6   https://www.forbes.com/2009/10/08/tamil-
tigers-rajiv-gandhi-opinions-contributors-sri-
lanka.html#4072179132ed

7   http://m.koreatimes.co.kr/phone/news/view.
        jsp?req_newsidx=47506

Sri Lankan Regime Backing Away from Conflict Resolution Vows

1   http://www.newindianexpress.com/world/2017/
        mar/29/sri-lankan-president-says-will-not-
        make-war-heroes-suspects-in-war-crime-
        cases-1587398.html

2   https://www.colombotelegraph.com/index.php/i-
        am-no-traitor-and-will-not-allow-federalism-
        says-sirisena/

3   http://www.asianmirror.lk/news/item/26242-
        president-sirisena-says-he-will-never-betray-the-
        country-by-introducing-federal-constitution

4   http://www.foxnews.com/world/2017/11/08/
        dozens-men-describe-rape-torture-by-sri-lanka-
        government.html

5   http://www.ctvnews.ca/world/dozens-of-
        men-describe-rape-and-torture-by-sri-lanka-
        government-1.3668288

Hindutva takes on Tamil Nationalism

1   https://www.jacobinmag.com/2015/09/
        india-general-strike-modi-kolkata-bjp-rss/

2   https://press.princeton.edu/titles/81.html

3   https://www.ndtv.com/tamil-nadu-news/video-
     of-kanchi-mutts-junior-pontiff-sitting-during-
     tamil-anthem-triggers-row-1804370

4   https://www.reuters.com/article/us-india-rss-
     specialreport/special-report-battling-for-indias-
     soul-state-by-state-idUSKCN0S700A20151013

5   http://indianexpress.com/article/opinion/bjp-
     has-many-plans-in-tamil-nadu-but-it-doesnt-
     know-tamil-politics-4815656/

Why Is Sri Lanka Defying the United Nations?

1   https://www.colombotelegraph.com/index.php/i-am-
     no-traitor-and-will-not-allow-federalism-says-sirisena/

2   http://www.thehindu.com/news/international/
     south-asia/un-defends-silence-on-genocide-in-
     sri-lanka-war-crimes-report/article7674861.ece

3   http://www.claritypress.com/Boyle-Tamil.html

4   Ibid

5   http://www.smh.com.au/entertainment/books/
     book-review-sri-lankas-secrets-by-trevor-grant-
     is-chronicle-of-genocide-20141201-11shqn.html

Why Colombo Remains a Challenge for New Delhi

1   https://www.opendemocracy.
     net/andreas-johansson/
     sri-lanka-local-elections-return-of-rajapaksa

2   http://www.thehindu.com/news/international/
     rajapaksa-backed-joint-opposition-moves-no-
     confidence-motion-against-pm-wickremesinghe/
     article23279061.ece

3   https://www.newsfirst.lk/2018/04/16-slfp-mps-
     cross-over-to-opposition-but-wont-join-jo-dilan-
     perera/

4   https://ipfs.io/ipfs/
     QmXoypizjW3WknFiJnKLwHCnL72vedxjQk
     DDP1mXWo6uco/wiki/South_Asian_foreign_
     policy_of_the_Narendra_Modi_government.
     html

5   https://economictimes.indiatimes.com/news/
     politics-and-nation/nothing-unusual-in-
     submarine-docking-at-sri-lanka-port-china/
     articleshow/45025664.cms?intenttarget=no

6   http://www.tehelka.com/2015/01/raw-led-to-
     mahinda-rajapaksas-defeat-in-sri-lanka-after-he-
     drove-wedge-between-india-china/?singlepage=1

7   http://www.thehindu.com/opinion/interview/
     rajapaksa-raw-not-government-conspired-
     against-me/article6987460.ece

8   https://www.smh.com.au/world/sri-lanka-
     election-shock-result-as-president-mahinda-
     rajapaksa-is-tossed-out-20150109-12l7nx.html

9   http://www.thehindu.com/webexclusives/
     antirajapaksa-vote-not-prosirisena-
     kumaravadivel-guruparan/article6771945.ece

10   http://www.atimes.com/article/sri-lanka-latest-
     victim-chinas-debt-trap-diplomacy/

11   https://www.forbes.com/2009/10/08/tamil-
     tigers-rajiv-gandhi-opinions-contributors-sri-
     lanka.html#4072179132ed

12   https://www.firstpost.com/world/indira-
     gandhi-helped-train-tamil-rebels-and-reaped-
     whirlwind-13913.html

13   http://news.rediff.com/slide-show/2009/aug/20/
     slide-show-1-how-india-helped-lanka-destroy-
     the-ltte.htm

14   https://www.colombotelegraph.com/index.php/
     india-will-be-there-whenever-you-need-us-if-
     you-do-things-our-way/

15 http://www.dailymirror.lk/article/india-
unsuited-to-play-mediator-due-to-tn-factor-
dayan-69451.html

16 https://asia.nikkei.com/Politics-Economy/Policy-
Politics/China-debt-worries-grow-in-Sri-Lanka-
as-ex-president-regains-clout

Can the Application of Universal Jurisdiction Foster Accountability in Sri Lanka?

1 http://colombogazette.com/wp-content/
uploads/2018/02/G1801853.pdf

2 http://www.un.org/News/dh/infocus/Sri_Lanka/
POE_Report_Full.pdf

3 http://www.bbc.com/news/world-asia-21873551

4 http://www.ohchr.org/EN/NewsEvents/Pages/
DisplayNews.aspx?NewsID=14447&LangID

5 https://www.reuters.com/article/
us-un-sri-lanka-rights/u-n-presses-sri-
lanka-to-meet-commitments-on-war-crimes-
investigations-reforms-idUSKBN16U2K3

6 https://news.un.org/en/story/2015/02/491192-
un-rights-chief-requests-one-time-only-deferral-
key-report-sri-lanka-conflict

7   https://lk.usembassy.gov/16731-2/

8   https://www.aljazeera.com/programmes/
     talktojazeera/2016/01/sri-lankan-president-
     allegations-war-crimes-160128150748006.html

9   https://www.colombotelegraph.com/index.php/i-
     am-no-traitor-and-will-not-allow-federalism-
     says-sirisena/

10   http://ww.trincocss.org\english\
     exclusive-interview-frances-harrison

11   http://www.ijrcenter.org/cases-before-national-
     courts/domestic-exercise-of-universal-
     jurisdiction/#gsc.tab=0

12   http://law.unimelb.edu.au/__data/assets/pdf_
     file/0010/1687249/Hood-and-Cormier.pdf

13   https://www.slguardian.org/alleged-sri-lankan-
     war-criminal-jagath-dias-withdrawn-as-
     diplomat-from-berlin/

14   http://www.bbc.com/news/world-asia-41039396

15   http://www.bbc.com/news/world-asia-41089396

16   http://www.trincocss.org/english/
     exclusive-interview-frances-harrison

Sri Lanka's Chinese Connection:
Beyond Bribes and Debts

1   https://www.nytimes.com/2018/06/25/world/
    asia/china-sri-lanka-port.html

2   http://colombogazette.com/2016/12/03/sri-lanka-to-
    buy-more-military-transport-planes-from-china/

3   http://articles.economictimes.indiatimes.
    com/2016-04-10/news/72209850_1_
    hambantota-port-maritime-silk-road-
    wickremesinghe

4   http://www.salem-news.com/articles/july162011/
    statesman-tamils-.php

5   http://www.salem-news.com/articles/july162011/
    statesman-tamils-.php

6   http://www.ft.lk/opinion/The-
    Troika%E2%80%93How-crucial-relations-with-
    India-were-managed-in-the-last-phase-of-the-
    separatist-war/14-656815

7   https://www.forbes.com/2009/10/08/tamil-
    tigers-rajiv-gandhi-opinions-contributors-sri-
    lanka.html#4072179132ed

8   https://www.forbes.com/2009/10/08/tamil-
    tigers-rajiv-gandhi-opinions-contributors-sri-
    lanka.html#4072179132ed

Unsilenced: Male Rape by the Sri Lankan Security Forces

1 http://www.itjpsl.com/reports/unsilenced

2 https://documents-dds-ny.un.org/doc/
UNDOC/GEN/G16/440/12/PDF/G1644012.
pdf?OpenElement

Sri Lanka's Tamil Cause, a Political Football?

1 https://www.deccanchronicle.com/nation/
current-affairs/200918/aiadmk-to-stage-protest-
against-dmk-on-september-25.html

2 https://indianexpress.com/article/india/
mahinda-rajapaksa-we-did-not-wage-ethnic-war-
action-was-not-against-tamils-5353467/

3 http://www.asianage.com/opinion/oped/120918/
at-last-delhi-asks-rajapaksa-for-a-dance.html

4 http://www.newindianexpress.com/states/
tamil-nadu/2018/sep/21/eelam-war-allegation-
tamil-nadu-bjp-chief-tamilisai-soundararajan-
joins-aiadmk-justifies-protest-1875088.html

5 https://www.thehindu.com/news/national/
tamil-nadu/jayalalithaa-moves-resolution-for-
international-probe-on-alleged-war-crimes-in-
sri-lanka/article7658982.ece

6   http://www.atimes.com/
     hindutva-takes-tamil-nationalism/

7   https://www.theweek.in/news/india/2018/07/28/
     Karunanidhi-A-blind-champion-of-Tamil-cause.
     html

Sri Lanka's Constitutional Crisis: The Geopolitical Dimension

1   https://www.onlanka.com/news/president-pm-
     in-heated-argument-over-east-terminal.html

2   https://ipfs.io/ipfs/QmXoypizjW3WknFiJnKLwH
     CnL72vedxjQkDDP1mXWo6uco/wiki/
     South_Asian_foreign_policy_of_the_
     Narendra_Modi_government.html

3   https://economictimes.indiatimes.com/news/
     politics-and-nation/nothing-unusual-in-
     submarine-docking-at-sri-lanka-port-china/
     articleshow/45025664.cms?intenttarget=no

4   http://www.atimes.com/why-colombo-
     remains-a-challenge-for-new-delhi/
     amp/

5   http://www.thehindu.com/opinion/interview/
     rajapaksa-raw-not-government-conspired-
     against-me/article6987460.ece

6   https://www.ibtimes.co.in/sri-lanka-buy-chinese-
    military-transport-aircraft-xian-y-20-are-they-
    good-workhorses-706965

7   https://www.ft.com/content/
    e150ef0c-de37-11e7-a8a4-0a1e63a52f9c

8   https://economynext.com/Sri_Lanka_
    President_rules_out_truck_with_Rajapaksa_
    faction-3-9710-.htm

9   https://www.thehindu.com/news/international/
    sri-lankan-president-sirisena-alleges-that-raw-is-
    plotting-his-assassination/article25241800.ece

10 https://twitter.com/nramind/status/1053130162122907649

11 https://www.thehindu.com/news/international/
    lanka-govt-rejects-reports-on-president-
    sirisenas-assassination-plot/article25249999.ece

12 https://www.financialexpress.com/world-news/
    chinese-president-xi-jinping-congratulates-
    newly-appointed-sri-lankan-prime-minister-
    mahinda-rajapaksa/1364433/

13 https://indianexpress.com/article/world/
    sri-lanka-mahinda-rajapakse-ranil-
    wickremesinghe-5420814/

14 https://www.youtube.com/watch?v=UatCLBqVBcw

15   https://www.tamilguardian.com/content/tamil-nadu-parties-condemn-rajapaksa-war-criminal

16   https://www.scmp.com/week-asia/politics/article/2170621/what-rajapaksas-return-means-china-india-tug-war-over-sri-lanka

17   https://www.scmp.com/news/asia/south-asia/article/2170593/us-urges-sri-lanka-immediately-reconvene-parliament-quell

An evaluation of Sri Lanka's Democratic Credentials

1   https://groundviews.org/2018/11/01/nailing-canards-why-president-sirisenas-actions-remain-illegal-unconstitutional-and-illegitimate/

2   https://groundviews.org/2018/11/01/nailing-canards-why-president-sirisenas-actions-remain-illegal-unconstitutional-and-illegitimate/

3   https://foreignpolicy.com/2018/11/16/asias-oldest-democracy-takes-a-hit/

4   https://epress.lib.uts.edu.au/journals/index.php/mcs/article/view/5143/5715

5   https://en.wikipedia.org/wiki/Ethnocracy

6   https://www.sciencedirect.com/science/article/pii/S0962629804000423

7   https://epress.lib.uts.edu.au/journals/index.php/
     mcs/article/view/5143/5715

How Sri Lanka Wards off War Crimes Investigators

1   https://www.hrw.org/asia/sri-lanka

2   https://www.colombotelegraph.com/index.php/i-
     am-no-traitor-and-will-not-allow-federalism-
     says-sirisena/

3   http://www.uktamilnews.com/?p=30988

4   http://www.jdslanka.org/index.php/news-
     features/politics-a-current-affairs/855-pm-ranil-
     wickremesinghe-requests

5   http://www.jdslanka.org/index.php/news-
     features/politics-a-current-affairs/855-pm-ranil-
     wickremesinghe-requests-tamils

6   https://thediplomat.com/2018/05/can-the-
     application-of-universal-jurisdiction-foster-
     accountability-in-sri-lanka/

7   https://www.aljazeera.com/news/2019/01/
     alleged-war-criminal-named-command-sri-
     lanka-army-190110161436349.html

8   https://www.icj.org/wp-content/
     uploads/2019/02/Sri-Lanka-Impunity-HRC40-
     Advocacy-non-legal-submission-2019-ENG.pdf

The Geopolitics of Sri Lanka's Transitional Justice

1   https://www.colombotelegraph.com/index.php/i-
     am-no-traitor-and-will-not-allow-federalism-
     says-sirisena/

2   http://www.jdslanka.org/index.php/news-
     features/politics-a-current-affairs/855-pm-ranil-
     wickremesinghe-requests-tamils

3   https://www.straitstimes.com/asia/south-asia/
     sri-lanka-tamils-demand-foreign-judges-in-war-
     crimes-probe

4   https://thediplomat.com/2016/04/samantha-
     power-misses-the-mark-on-sri-lanka-again/

5   https://www.hrw.org/report/2018/10/09/
     why-cant-we-go-home/
     military-occupation-land-sri-lanka

6   https://twitter.com/USAmbSLM/
     status/1090084121806802944

7   https://www.thestar.com/news/
     canada/2013/10/07/harper_makes_good_on_
     threat_to_boycott_sri_lanka_over_human_
     rights_violations.html

8   https://www.bbc.com/news/av/world-asia-24967501/cameron-calls-for-war-crimes-inquiry-in-sri-lanka

9   https://www.telegraph.co.uk/news/worldnews/asia/srilanka/10494147/US-warns-Sri-Lanka-over-failure-to-investigate-war-crimes.html

10   https://www.scmp.com/news/asia/article/1420656/sri-lanka-bars-us-envoy-president-lashes-out-proposed-un-war-crimes

11   http://m.koreatimes.co.kr/phone/news/view.jsp?req_newsidx=47506

12   https://www.govinfo.gov/content/pkg/CPRT-111SPRT53866/html/CPRT-111SPRT53866.htm

13   https://www.un.org/News/dh/infocus/Sri_Lanka/POE_Report_Full.pdf

Sri Lanka's Muslims Bloodied by Buddhism

1   https://www.telegraph.co.uk/news/2019/06/03/every-muslim-minister-sri-lanka-resigns-following-crackdown/

2   http://www.reuters.com/article/us-sri-lanka-doctor-insight/unsubstantiated-claims-muslim-doctor-sterilized-women-raise-tensions-in-sri-lanka-idUSKCN1T71HS

3   http://srilankabrief.org/2019/06/sri-lanka-
     arresting-first-and-calling-for-complaints-later-
     mockery-of-justice-say-le

4   https://www.reuters.com/article/us-sri-lanka-
     blasts-resignation/sri-lanka-muslim-officials-
     quit-in-solidarity-with-minister-accused-of-
     islamist-ties-idUSKCN1T421D

5   https://www.facebook.com/
     RauffHakeemOfficial/videos/an-interview-given-
     to-australia-abc-radio/2312915502300188/

US Push for New Military Agreement Runs into Fierce Opposition in Sri Lanka

1   https://www.scmp.com/week-asia/geopolitics/
     article/3020308/us-naval-base-rumours-sri-
     lanka-spark-alarm-washington-and

2   https://economictimes.indiatimes.com/news/
     international/world-news/mike-pompeo-cancels-
     sri-lanka-visit-over-anti-us-base-sentiments/
     articleshow/69935922.cms

3   https://www.indepthnews.net/index.php/the-
     world/asia-pacific/2785-sri-lanka-s-strategic-
     location-incites-us-china-rivalry

4   https://economictimes.indiatimes.com/
news/international/world-news/mike-
pompeo-cancels-sri-lanka-visit-over-anti-
us-base-sentiments/articleshow/69935922.
cms?utm_source=contentofinterest&utm_
medium=text&utm_campaign=cpps

5   https://www.reuters.com/article/us-sri-lanka-
usa/sri-lanka-pm-says-still-in-talks-with-us-on-
military-cooperation-pact-idUSKCN1U61L9

6   https://www.reuters.com/article/us-sri-lanka-
usa/sri-lanka-pm-says-still-in-talks-with-us-on-
military-cooperation-pact-idUSKCN1U61L9

7   https://www.colombotelegraph.com/index.php/
us-sl-draft-sofa-reveals-american-plan-to-turn-
sl-into-military-colon

8   http://colombopage.com/archive_19A/
Jul02_1562006029CH.php

9   https://colombogazette.com/2019/07/17/
us-denies-funding-regime-change-in-sri-lanka/

10   https://colombogazette.com/2019/07/17/
us-denies-funding-regime-change-in-sri-lanka/

11   https://www.scmp.com/news/asia/south-asia/
article/2095795/sri-lankan-peacekeepers-stand-
accused-running-child-sex-ring

Sri Lanka's 'Victor's Peace' and the Way Forward

1   Damien Kingsbury, "Sri Lanka's military showdown: is this it?", 23rd April 2009, http://www.crikey.com.au/2009/04/23/sri-lanka%E2%80%99s-military-showdown-is-this-it/?wpmp_switcher=mobile,

2   https://www.colombotelegraph.com/index.php/sri-lanka-is-one-of-the-peaceful-stable-and-democratically-secured-countries-in-the-wo

3   https://www.newsfirst.lk/2019/05/19/the-decade-of-peace-we-celebrate-in-triumph/

4   https://graphics.reuters.com/SRI%20LANKA-BLASTS/010091JW299/index.html

5   Andrea Iff "Constitutional Accommodation vs. Integration in Sri Lanka", in Ana Pararajasingham (ed) "Sri Lanka: 60 Years of Independence and Beyond", Centre for Just Peace and Democracy, Emmenbrucke,2009,p36

6   Charles Ponnuthurai Sarvan in the Colombo Telegraph , 5 May 2018 https://www.colombotelegraph.com/index.php/the-island-story-a-short-history-of-sri-lanka/

7   "The Forever War?: Military Control in Sri
     Lanka's North" Crisis Group, 25 March 2014
     http://blog.crisisgroup.org/asia/2014/03/25/the-
     forever-war-military-control-in-sri-lankas-north/

8   S. I. Keethaponcalan, TNA's Sambanthan
     Ready For Armed Struggle?, *Colombo
     Telegraph* 7 August 2019 https://www.
     colombotelegraph.com/index.php/
     tnas-sambanthan-ready-for-armed-struggle/

9   SRI LANKA: RECHARTING U.S. STRATEGY
     AFTER THE WAR , December 7, 2009
     https://www.govinfo.gov/content/pkg/CPRT-
     111SPRT53866/html/CPRT-111SPRT53866.htm